Workforce Development

Workforce Development

Guidelines for Community College Professionals

Edited by
William J. Rothwell
Patrick E. Gerity
Vernon L. Carraway

ROWMAN & LITTLEFIELD
Lanham • Boulder • New York • London

Published by Rowman & Littlefield
An imprint of The Rowman & Littlefield Publishing Group, Inc.
4501 Forbes Boulevard, Suite 200, Lanham, Maryland 20706
www.rowman.com

6 Tinworth Street, London SE11 5AL, United Kingdom

Copyright © 2020 by William J. Rothwell, Patrick E. Gerity, and Vernon L. Carraway

All rights reserved. No part of this book may be reproduced in any form or by any electronic or mechanical means, including information storage and retrieval systems, without written permission from the publisher, except by a reviewer who may quote passages in a review.

British Library Cataloguing in Publication Information Available

Library of Congress Control Number: 2019957493
ISBN 978-1-4758-4933-2 (cloth: alk. paper)
ISBN 978-1-4758-4934-9 (pbk. : alk. paper)
ISBN 978-1-4758-4935-6 (electronic)

∞ ™ The paper used in this publication meets the minimum requirements of American National Standard for Information Sciences Permanence of Paper for Printed Library Materials, ANSI/NISO Z39.48-1992.

William J. Rothwell dedicates this book to his wife, Marcelina V. Rothwell, his son Froilan Perucho, his daughter Candice Szczesny, his grandsons Aden and Gabriel, and his granddaughter Freya.

Patrick E. Gerity dedicates this book to his wife Cyn, his daughters Rya, Jaissa, and Shayla; also to the leaders who dedicate their careers to community college workforce and economic development.

Vernon L. Carraway dedicates this book to his loving and supportive wife Charlotte E. Watson Carraway, their children Quincy. Langston, Leah and Dorrian; and to all the students, from whom I have learned more than they will ever know.

Contents

Preface	ix
Acknowledgments	xi
Introduction	xiii

Part I: External Issues Affecting Community College Workforce Development — 1

1. Labor Market Information for Data-Driven Decision Making at Community Colleges — 3
   Alex Cooley
2. Strategic Partnerships: Maximizing the Benefits of Partnerships — 11
   Alicia R. Hooks
3. Relationships Matter: Building Community Partnerships for Workforce Development — 17
   Robin Cole Jr.
4. Building an Agile Community College: Strategic Transformation and Embedding Innovation as a Competency — 27
   Sue Ellspermann
5. Rising with the Machines: Embracing Opportunity—and Living Your Values—in an Age of Transformation — 41
   Lee D. Lambert

Part II: Internal Issues Affecting Community College Workforce Development — 49

6. Making a Case for Workforce Development — 51
   Ty A. Stone

7 Understanding Equity and its Importance in Developing the
   Workforce of the Future   57
   Angela Davis, Susan Paris, and Jairo McMican

8 Technological Change: Human Adaptation Through Effective
   Learning   65
   Stephen R. Catt

9 Embedded Industry Credentials: A Measure of Student Success   73
   Bryan Albrecht and Matt Janisin

10 Learning While Working   81
   Paul Schreffler

11 Finance and Budgeting for Workforce Professionals   109
   John Will

Part III: Special Issues Affecting Community College Workforce Development   121

12 Factors Influencing the Retention and Persistence of African
   American and Latino Male STEM Students in Community College   123
   Michael C. Wood

13 Dealing with the Changing Face of Workforce Development   141
   Victor Rodgers

14 Conceptualizing Future Competencies Needed by Community
   College Workforce Development Practitioners   153
   William J. Rothwell, Patrick E. Gerity, and Vernon L. Carraway

Appendix A: Rating Your Competence in Workforce Development   161

Appendix B: Selected Resources for Community College Workforce
   Development Professionals   167

Index   171

About the Editors and Contributors   179

Preface

Community college workforce developers often secure their jobs without advance training in their roles. Consequently, there remains a gap between the role they play and the role they could play if they were better informed. This book is intended to provide a grounding for community college workforce developers—and others in community colleges who bear workforce development responsibilities. These "others" may include Boards of Director members, Community College Presidents, Deans and Department Heads and even Community College faculty members. So, the key audiences for this book include community college workforce developers and others who bear workforce development responsibilities.

The book opens with an Introduction. Its goal is to help you zero in on what you most want to know about in the book and find it right away. Use it to reflect on your personal and professional development needs as a workforce development professional and on the needs of your institution.

This book is divided into three parts.

Part I focuses on External Issues Affecting Community College Workforce Development. Chapter 1 reviews the importance of grounding community college efforts on labor market information. Effective programming is based on what it takes to help workers secure and maintain employment, and that information comes from labor market data. Chapter 2 examines the importance to community colleges of strategic partnerships. Related to Chapter 2, Chapter 3 looks at ways to build community partnerships for workforce development. Chapter 4 examines the popular topic of agility and how it applies to strategic transformation and innovation in the community college context. Chapter 5 explains how values will shape a community college and how important it is to clarify and sustain values in an age when machines—

robots and artificial intelligence—are on the rise and humanity may be declining in workplace importance.

Part II focuses on Internal Issues Affecting Community College Workforce Development. What is the role of workforce development in community colleges? Chapter 6 focuses on that question. What leadership is needed in community colleges in the future? Chapter 7 addresses that question, looking also at how important it is to gain the competitive advantages provided by a commitment to diversity, equity and inclusion. Chapter 8 explores the impact of technological change on learning, a topic that will undoubtedly shape community college workforce development heavily in the future. Chapter 9 shifts to educational programming, looking at embedded credentials and how they can help students of the future get and keep the skills they need for employment. Chapter 10 continues in the same vein, looking at cooperative education and ways that students can learn while they work. Chapter 11 concludes part II by treating finance and budgeting issues for workforce development professionals, an area where many workforce development professionals could stand to improve.

Part III focuses on Special Issues Affecting Community College Workforce Development. Special topics include "Factors Influencing the Retention and Persistence of African American and Latino Males in Community College and STEM," the title of Chapter 12. That chapter is followed by a look at Work Keys, covered in Chapter 13. Work Keys is a popular approach for examining employers' workforce development needs so that those needs can be met by community college workforce developers. Chapter 14 concludes part III and ends the book by "Conceptualizing Future Competencies Needed by Community College Workforce Development Practitioners."

Acknowledgments

Editing a book is like taking a long ocean voyage. Finding willing authors is like finding a crew for the ship. Giving the authors careful instructions is akin to the challenge facing a ship's captain, where effective leadership means telling people clearly how they should play their parts. Shaping the manuscript occurs in a series of steps, beginning with a process of reviewing chapter outlines, providing feedback about them, soliciting chapter rough drafts, providing feedback on those, and finally securing final chapter drafts and bringing them into compliance with the publisher's requirements.

Many people helped to bring this volume about. We wish to thank them. That includes the chapter authors and our own review board of people who examined the book and offered suggestions. Reviewers included Steve Mitchell, Christian LaGarde, and Jennifer Worth, whose biosketches are included in the contributor section. We would like to give a very special thanks to Jennifer Worth, senior vice president of workforce and economic development, American Association of Community Colleges, who is a driving force behind community college workforce and economic development both nationally and globally.

Introduction

Consider this tool the introduction to this book. Use it as a diagnostic tool to help you assess what you most want to know about workforce development in community colleges—and where you can find it *fast* in this book.

THE ORGANIZER

Directions

Read each item in the Organizer below. Circle a *True (T)*, a *Not Applicable (N/A)*, or *False (F)* in the left column opposite each item. Spend about 10 minutes on the Organizer. Be honest! Think of workforce development as you experience it—and not what others say it should be.

When you finish, score and interpret the results using the instructions appearing at the end of the Organizer. Then be prepared to share your responses with others you know to help you think about what you most want to learn about. If you would like to learn more about one item below, refer to the number in the right column to find the chapter in this book in which the subject is discussed.

The Questions

Circle your response for each item below.

Does your community college:

				Chapter covered
Y	N/A	N	1. Use labor market data to guide program planning and discussions with local employers?	1
Y	N/A	N	2. Have a systematic approach to forming local partnerships?	2
Y	N/A	N	3. Have ways to build partnerships in your community?	3
Y	N/A	N	4. Take steps to transform strategically to meet needs of those you serve?	4
Y	N/A	N	5. Clarify your institutional values and take steps to act in alignment with them?	5
Y	N/A	N	6. Persuade others about the importance of workforce development?	6
Y	N/A	N	7. Demonstrate support for equity efforts?	7
Y	N/A	N	8. Help learners keep pace with the impact that technology has had, and is having, on learning to keep pace with present/future work requirements?	8
Y	N/A	N	9. Use embedded credentials?	9
Y	N/A	N	10. Use effective work-based learning practices?	10
Y	N/A	N	11 Develop budgets that are based on good financial practices and are aligned with organizational and community priorities?	11
Y	N/A	N	12. Address factors influencing the retention and persistence of African American and Latino males in community college and Science, Technology, Engineering and Mathematics (STEM)?	12
Y	N/A	N	13. Explore using Work Keys for Workforce Development?	13
Y	N/A	N	14. Take steps to conceptualize future competencies needed by community college workforce development practitioners and worked to develop them?	14
Y	N/A	N	15. Take steps to conceptualize present competencies needed by community college workforce development practitioners and worked to develop them?	Appendix I
Y	N/A	N	16. Explore resources to assist in workforce development?	Appendix II
				____ Total

Scoring and Interpreting the Organizer

Give yourself *1 point for each Y* and a *0 for each N or N/A* listed above. Total the points from the *Y* column and place the sum in the line opposite to the word **TOTAL** above. Then interpret your score as follows:

Score

15–16 points   Congratulations! *Give your organization a grade of A.*

13–14 points   *Give your organization a grade of B.* Your organization is making progress but still has room for improvement in its commitment to workforce development.

11–12 points   *Give your organization a grade of C.* Your organization is about average, and that means your organization should take steps to improve its commitment to workforce development.

9–10 points   *Give your organization a grade of D.* Your organization is below average. That means you need to play catch up to improve the institution's commitment to workforce development.

0–8 points   *Give your organization a grade of F.* Take immediate steps to improve the organization's commitment to workforce development.

Part I

External Issues Affecting Community College Workforce Development

Chapter One

Labor Market Information for Data-Driven Decision Making at Community Colleges

Alex Cooley

Data-driven decision-making has become increasingly popular worldwide, in both business and higher education. Although labor market information (LMI) has existed for decades, technology has improved our ability to quickly gather, analyze, and share data with stakeholders. The internet has increased the accessibility of LMI, and its popularity in higher education has grown exponentially over the past several years.

This chapter will discuss what LMI is, the various uses of LMI in higher education, and how Northern Virginia Community College (NOVA) uses LMI to inform curriculum decisions, provide career awareness to students, and build relationships with regional employers and stakeholders.

DEFINING LABOR MARKET INFORMATION

Labor market information (LMI), sometimes referred to as labor market intelligence, is a collection of economic, demographic, and education data used to describe local, regional, state, or national economies relative to the workforce. Labor market researchers are data analysts and economists who study the job market to make informed decisions within their organization.

LMI is used in both the public and private sector to study the workforce and population. Organizations that utilize LMI include but are not limited to government organizations, employers, real estate firms, nonprofit organizations, K–12 and higher education institutions, economic and workforce development agencies, and policy research centers. LMI is particularly helpful in decisions related to career exploration and discovery, workforce planning, program and curriculum development, policy planning and implementation, and economic development.

The three types of LMI data (economic, demographic, and education) can tell a story about a particular economy, predict future workforce supply and demand, or address specific questions related to the labor market. Economic data, such as the unemployment rate, total employment, salaries, and number of businesses, are the primary sources for LMI. Demographic and education data are most often used to contextualize economic data points for the broader region.

Examples of demographic data include items like the population numbers and information on the housing market, while education data highlights student enrollments and completions at postsecondary institutions. Labor market data can also help answer questions such as: What is the market salary for a particular industry or occupation? Which occupations and industries are projected to grow in the future? What is the typical education level of workers in a particular job? What is the unemployment rate?

USING LABOR MARKET INFORMATION

Now that we have defined LMI, it is important to understand how it is gathered, analyzed, and disseminated. The LMI system in the United States has three primary components: data collection, data analysis, and data reporting and consumption.

First, various government agencies and organizations collect data at the local, state, and federal levels, primarily through survey data (i.e., the Census) or through third-party vendors that analyze online job advertisements. Second, economists, data analysts, and researchers at the various organizations analyze the information. Third, these organizations publish their LMI findings for the public. LMI can be presented to users in a variety of ways, through reports, brochures, websites, and presentations.

LMI data is often communicated through charts, infographics, and other data visualization methods to present data in a useful, informative, and concise way. Popular examples of data visualization tools include Microsoft Office, Tableau, and Google Charts.

There are a variety of professional organizations and membership networks in the United States dedicated to promoting the use of LMI. The Council for Community and Economic Research (C2ER) is a membership trade organization that provides training opportunities, consulting services, networking events, and various other support activities and programs for labor market researchers and organizations that utilize LMI. Affiliates of C2ER include the Association for Public Data Users (APDU), the Center for

Regional Economic Competitiveness (CREC), and the Labor Market Information (LMI) Institute.

These organizations offer numerous resources to their members, including the Cost of Living Index, the State Economic Expenditures Database, and the State Business Incentives Database.

LABOR MARKET INFORMATION (LMI) AND COMMUNITY COLLEGES

LMI usage in higher education has gained popularity in recent years, at both four-year institutions and community colleges across the country. Data that drive decision-making has become an essential component of the global economy. While much of the LMI research at four-year institutions focuses on national trends and research, such as the Center for Education and the Workforce at Georgetown University, the LMI research conducted at the community college level is largely geared toward solving local or regional challenges.

Community colleges are also using LMI data, not only for program and curriculum evaluation, but also to provide real-time career information to students. Many colleges employ full-time staff members to perform data analysis of LMI. Examples of community colleges with robust LMI research capabilities include the Dallas Community College District and the State of California Centers of Excellence for Labor Market Information.

The use of third-party vendors to provide career awareness information to students is also popular among colleges nationwide, through various programs such as Career Coach from EMSI and Career Insight from Burning Glass Technologies. Programs like these bring real-time LMI data to students directly through a web-based platform, allowing students to determine career outcomes for various programs of study to help them make informed career decisions.

LABOR MARKET INFORMATION (LMI) AT NORTHERN VIRGINIA COMMUNITY COLLEGE

The northern Virginia region, located in the suburbs of Washington, D.C., has a robust economy with a diverse and educated population. Northern Virginia Community College serves approximately 85,000 degree-seeking and workforce students per year in a region of approximately 2.5 million residents. NOVA is the largest institution of higher education in the Commonwealth of Virginia, and one of the largest community colleges in the nation.

In 2016, NOVA recognized that there was no regional entity providing LMI to the community. Although a few organizations were performing this work at a local level, there was no primary coordinator and provider for all regional labor market data. NOVA saw this unmet need as a strategic opportunity that the College was uniquely positioned to address, in part because of the College's regional footprint across northern Virginia. NOVA now provides LMI to all stakeholders in the region, including local governments, the K–12 school districts, workforce and economic development agencies, and community-based organizations.

NOVA prioritizes serving the local community by providing access to quality, affordable education to students and by connecting employers with talent to meet their business' needs. Each year, more than 2,000 employers in the region connect with NOVA to recruit students for employment and experiential learning opportunities, including recruitment for full-time and part-time positions, attendance at career services events, and internship and apprenticeship opportunities. By using LMI, NOVA can better position students for careers in high-wage, in-demand jobs and provide employers with access to a robust talent pool.

While the economy in northern Virginia is strong on many indicators, one significant challenge remains: many jobs in high-demand areas like information technology and healthcare are unfilled. While technology workers make up about 9.5 percent of the region's workforce—three times greater than the national average—technology jobs consistently make up more than 25 percent of all job opportunities advertised by employers in the region. Although colleges in the region have thousands of students graduating with technology degrees each year, the employer demand for these workers continues to exceed the region's supply.

For northern Virginia to remain economically competitive, NOVA and other educational institutions must build the talent pipeline that employers need. LMI allows the College to understand the job market, adapt quickly to its changing dynamics, engage more employers, and educate students about employment opportunities.

NOVA takes the guesswork out of workforce development by providing the community with access to LMI. Through real-time job market analytics and economic modeling, we help illustrate northern Virginia's economic landscape, including market conditions and growth rates, skill shortages, and talent demands. Our goal is to respond to immediate labor market needs, mitigate skills gaps before they occur, and build talent development strategies based on labor market projections. The result is a data-driven talent development system that adapts to macro and micro economic trends and works for our region's businesses, students, and community.

NOVA LMI: DATA FOR GOOD. DATA FOR BUSINESS. DATA FOR LEARNING

NOVA conducts research on the labor market for three primary purposes: to provide data for public good, data for business, and data for learning.

First, NOVA provides data for the public good. Our research is meant for public consumption. The College provides LMI to the public through publications like career ladders, economic dashboards, and interactive web tools to inform and educate community members about the regional economy.

The northern Virginia region has a critical need to develop the talent pipeline in fields like information technology and health care, where many jobs go unfilled. Currently, the region does not produce enough graduates in these fields to meet the needs of employers. Therefore, career awareness at the K–12 level is especially important. Through LMI data, students can make informed decisions about their career paths, providing them with a clear pathway from high school to the workplace.

Career awareness through LMI may also help students eliminate a particular career path or allow them to consider a career they did not know existed or had not previously considered. Additionally, by supporting students in their effort to make informed decisions, we can reduce the amount of their educational debt. Students may also be equipped to pursue better opportunities for them that meet their educational needs, such as pursuing a technical degree or short-term training program, instead of a four-year degree. LMI can also be useful to other populations of the workforce, like workers looking to change career fields, those looking to up-skill or obtain an industry certification and transitioning military service members.

Second, we provide data for business. The College engages continually and thoughtfully with the regional business community as part of its strategic vision and mission. The relationship between employers and NOVA is a win-win; companies use the research to understand the talent pipeline, and NOVA hears from employers about which skills and credentials they are seeking from the talent pool to meet their needs.

It is important to substantiate the data provided by the Bureau of Labor Statistics and other sources with employers themselves. LMI data provides a good starting point, but vetting the information with regional employers allows the College to understand regional employer needs beyond what the data alone can demonstrate.

NOVA also provides LMI to employers to support their success. The College acts as a consultant with regional employers, using LMI data, to assist employers with attracting and retaining workers. Examples of this kind of partnership include performing market salary assessments for an employer, providing reports on industry credentials or skills, and providing industry and occupation projection demands for the region. The College also works with local, regional, and state economic development agencies and chambers of commerce to assist with regional business retention, expansion, and attraction efforts.

Partnerships between NOVA and employers allow for strategic working relationships and innovative new programs. New programs include corporate sponsorships, apprenticeship programs, customized workforce training, and work-based learning and career opportunities for students. Collaborations between the College and regional employers can address specific needs. For instance, in 2018, NOVA collaborated with Amazon Web Services (AWS) to create a first-of-its-kind cloud computing specialization within the Information Systems Technology degree program. The northern Virginia region is home to the headquarters of AWS and many other employers who require workers who are skilled in data center management and cloud-computing. AWS coordinated with NOVA to create curriculum mapped to skills and competency-based credentials in cloud computing. The College used LMI in consultation with AWS to determine the appropriate skills and credentials for the new course offerings.

Lastly, we employ data for learning. NOVA uses LMI to make informed decisions about curriculum and programs at the college. Trends from the Bureau of Labor Statistics, as well as job postings data derived from proprietary sources, allow the College to forecast the needs of the business community.

Forecasting business needs provide guidance to the College in structuring new programs, and modifying, updating, or eliminating obsolete curriculum. This is particularly true for industry credentials and emerging skills in high-demand fields like information technology and health care, where the needs of businesses evolve much faster than higher education. By keeping a pulse on regional employer demands, NOVA can quickly implement new course offerings and industry certifications before the skill shortage becomes critical.

Additionally, LMI allows the College to engage meaningfully with employers who have hiring needs, to facilitate the connection between the region's job opportunities and our students. The College's primary focus is to serve the educational needs of the community, and LMI data allows us to keep up with the evolving needs of employers and adapt quickly to the rapidly changing business environment.

CONCLUSION

The use of LMI at Northern Virginia Community College has been a critical component in the College's business engagement. LMI provides a foundation for meaningful conversations with employers about their needs, and how the college can help industry address those needs today and for the workforce needs of tomorrow. Recently, the college used LMI to assist in recruiting and engaging business leaders to serve on the college's industry advisory boards, which were overhauled to include employers offering job and internship opportunities to NOVA students.

As a regional resource for LMI, the college has been fortunate to participate in numerous economic development activities, including the winning Amazon HQ2 bid, to highlight the data story of the region's strong workforce.

LMI is increasingly important for community colleges to incorporate into their strategic vision and mission. LMI empowers community colleges to address the needs of regional employers and ensure student career success upon graduation. As colleges across the nation work to align economic data with education pathways and employer needs, trends in the use of LMI will continue to grow.

Chapter Two

Strategic Partnerships

Maximizing the Benefits of Partnerships

Alicia R. Hooks

> "When private sector, government, social, and philanthropic leaders apply innovative partnerships and technologies to address social challenges and build sustainable communities, the impact is multiplied."—Tae Yoo

Workforce development leaders play a significant role in multiplying the impact of strategic partnerships. When equipped with the right competencies, data, and organizational placement, the department plays a very powerful role in the success of the students, the college, business/industry, the community, and all other stakeholders. Some institutions support the workforce development department with more than sufficient resources and receive a reciprocal response from the community, business/industry, and local/state/federal resources to ensure total and complete departmental and community success due to the level of importance and community impact.

Unfortunately, not all community colleges place their workforce development departments strategically within the hierarchy of the institution to support the department and maximize the benefits for the college, students, community, business and industry stakeholders. Handled strategically, workforce development can produce more than partnerships resulting in simple job opportunities for students and training opportunities for the college. Those types of partnerships in general are easy to obtain.

However, strategic partnerships providing continual exponential benefits to all partners involved are unique and of a necessity. The competencies, data, and organizational placement needed to identify, form, develop, and expand strategic partnerships providing maximum benefits to all involved is the topic of this chapter.

COMPETENCIES

While community college workforce departments focus on identifying, categorizing, and training competencies, there is additionally a need to identify what competencies support the workforce development leader. Too often, in the community college arena, the workforce department is understaffed resulting in the leadership performing the same or similar tasks as the remaining staff. Because of this, workforce leadership are not afforded the opportunity to embrace and engraft the competencies used to expand opportunities for more significant and strategic partnerships.

Many are aware of this reality. The question is, how should this barrier be addressed? Who has the time, effort, energy, and luxury to develop additional competencies while meeting the current demands of the workforce leadership position and filling the gap of supporting positions? However, how can the program grow in the absence of those competencies? What specifically are the competencies that shift a workforce program into an outcome driven set of systems that breeds momentum?

The competencies supporting the workforce development leader in the identification, forming, development, and expansion of strategic partnerships providing maximum benefits to all parties involved are different from the various workforce development staff members. The leadership competencies include, but are not limited to, the following:

The workforce development leader must possess a variety of competencies primarily for the purposes of engaging in a form of mental image bending. The leader must be able to bend their mental image of what is even possible given a certain set of circumstances and limited resources. To be the catalyst between the community, the college, and business/industry, the workforce leader must have a level of foresight which goes beyond average predictive analytics.

The workforce development leader is, in a sense, an alchemist who must mix elements not normally thought to produce a certain outcome, and cause a transmutation leading to amazing, innovating, and sustainable results benefitting businesses, communities, and the college. Their mental image of what is possible must be flexible enough to bend to meet the needs of multiple

Table 2.1. Competencies Needed by Workforce Development Leaders

• Higher level negotiation skills	• Flexibility
• Grant writing	• Risk taker
• Sales & Marketing	• Rapport builder
• Supply chain operations	• Governmental relations (local/state/federal)
• Entrepreneurial mindset	
• Business analysis (ROI, processes, etc.)	• Innovation
	• And more…

stakeholders. If the workforce development leader's focus is on handling day-to-day tasks generally delegated to other managers or subordinate staff, these innovations become more difficult. The popular phrase, "*A bend in the road is not the end of the road, unless you refuse to turn*" comes to mind.

The workforce development leader must have the ability to take limited resources and increased need, combine it with the opportunity for partnerships, and identify a strategic partnership supplying the increased need while satisfying the need for all parties involved. This is additionally why specialized negotiation skills work best as opposed to simple contract closing skills.

Akin to negotiation competencies are sales skills. Sales skills involve an element of predictability and a logical process when conducted correctly. There is a huge difference when transitioning from working in the business world, working in a congressional office, and working in academia. The business and political arenas are big in their knowledge of sales and negotiation. Even to the point of being trained in hostage negotiations for business deals!

Academia appears to put very little emphasis on sales and negotiation competencies and trainings. Businesses and politicians know that this drives revenue...the very thing many colleges and workforce departments need more of! It seems logical that since the workforce leaders have built the relationships with business/industry and the community, they would be encouraged and supported in building those competencies.

Similar are the competencies involved with the entrepreneurial mindset referred to as effectuation logic. Workforce development leaders need the competencies of effectual logic. This logic process supports innovation, the use of limited resources, how to best identify and use strategic partnerships, how to handle the failures when they come, and turning experimental processes into operational procedures for delegation and management.

Throughout the process of identifying and maximizing strategic partnerships, competencies include the ability to be flexible or requisite variety. Requisite variety is a basic premise or belief the leader adopts that whomever is the most flexible in a system controls that system. The workforce development leader, having the ability to be flexible to meet the needs of the college, community, students and stakeholders in a way in which maximizes benefits for all, is an exponential win.

Effectual logic involves a way of thinking which supports the creation of a non-existent market to meet a newly arising need. This as opposed to waiting until the need has been established as often occurs in academia. When a college waits too long to respond to the needs of the market, the market will find another way to meet its own need. Because of this, the workforce leader must have the competency or ability to think entrepreneurially...to think through the entrepreneurial processes. This involves strategic partnerships, not the leader in isolation. Part of this process involves connecting and involving the community.

When this writer was working on my dissertation and studying nascent entrepreneurs, a common theme emerged regarding new ventures and sustainability. That theme involved the community. The new business venture had to be involved in the community and get the community involved with them. Likewise, the workforce development leader can extend their limited staff by utilizing the community as a resource through a strategic process that breeds sustainable outcomes. Identifying the resources must be done creatively and iteratively. It is not a rigid process. To identify the right partners is to have the right focus of the needs of all involved.

Without being flexible, academia can easily focus solely on the needs of the institution versus joining in on the pains and limitations the business is experiencing. The institution, with all its subject matter experts and top-level equipment, is more than equipped to identify and address all the needs of business and industry to assist in its sustainability and growth. However, educational institutions most often than not focus most on placing students and identifying training opportunities the businesses may have. There is so much more and so many more opportunities to create strategic partnerships, which breed exponential success for all parties involved. The competencies need activating supported by the data.

DATA

Workforce development leaders cannot monitor what they cannot measure. The leaders themselves must be able to produce and at least interpret the data. An attempt to interpret data produced for other reasons or to extrapolate data not derived for the purpose of workforce analytics may not produce sufficient data to provide an accurate representation to make sound decisions for a leader.

Knowing an area anecdotally speaks to the leader's power of observation; supporting it with data speaks to their quality of leadership. Feelings are never a valid basis for fact. Economic scans, program demand gap analysis, graduate career placement analysis and more fall within the realm of the analytics of the workforce development department leader.

Leaders use analyzed and synthesized data to understand the entire supply chain of services offered including where program gaps exist. Examining what employers are looking for and how the floor supervisor's needs differ from the human resources' posted job description and how that differs from the President's vision of the company's culture is a key performance indicator for a successful strategic partnership. Leaders identify key performance indicators through the effective utilization of the appropriate competencies and the accurate use and implementation of the complete data, not simply a partial view.

Workforce development leaders must know what data to collect analyze and implement change upon, however, they must also train the staff on what the data means. The entire staff must be able to look at the aggregate data and understand how the data applies to their area of operations so they may take responsibility and ownership for change. Additionally, this data assists with grant writing and grant searches. Instead on limiting grant searches to workforce, labor or similar areas, recognizing trends in the data will allow the leader to broaden the search to certain areas, populations, industries impacted, etc. . . . that are revealed.

Additionally, trends in data allow for forecasting which bring an awareness for foundational support, increase sponsorships and public/private/partnerships (P3s). In general, leaders use data to support results and reduce reasons. Lastly, leaders also use data as an element of predictability in trendsetting. Academic institutions tend to follow trends when it comes to business and industry versus setting trends. If a college is merely obtaining data from a single source, caution is advised. I have personally witnessed advice being provided through economic development initiatives which were not sufficiently engaged in community development resulting in mal-advisement to the college. Community colleges are very different that many four-year institutions in that graduates of community colleges tend to remain in the community. Graduates from Universities tend to come from outside the area and leave the area following graduation.

Therefore, community colleges find a greater return from their investment in the community and play a key role in balancing between business/industry, the community, and can be the catalyst to assist in the development of both. By placing most of their focus on data pertaining to new business development and meeting the needs of potential new businesses, they can potentially be damaging their own plan for sustainability. Using effectual logic competencies, community college leaders can establish strategic partnerships to be ahead of the curve and set the trends versus follow the trends.

ORGANIZATIONAL PLACEMENT

For a community college to be a trendsetter, it must be able to respond quickly and engage in a strategic partnership. Business and industry must be nimble in their responses to the marketplace. As such, they are not always able to wait for one to three years to wait on the world of academia, which has its own separate set of processes. For this reason, college leadership may consider placing the workforce development department within the academic organization in such a way it is able to respond quickly to business and industry.

When identifying an innovative approach to a solution for a particular industry, the business may need to begin within thirty days. The workforce development leader will need to have the workforce development department located in the organizational chart in such a way that they have the authority to reach out to all parties involved and to make the necessary decisions to meet the business's needs. Additionally, when the business wants to respond with large funding donations and sponsorships for specialized programs, workforce development leaders must handle this in a way that is easy for the business and in a celebratory fashion. The workforce development leader needs the latitude and organizational chart placement in order to do so.

Colleges having greater levels of success have had their workforce development leaders close to the presidents or the financial officers of the college. When the workforce leader is not answering to someone with a corporate, business or entrepreneurial understanding, progress tends to be halted for lack of understanding of accelerated operational processes which normally occur in the business arena.

CONCLUSION

Community colleges are unique because most of their graduates tend to stay in the community as opposed to four-year universities receiving students from around the nation who tend to return to their home state or travel to the location of the best career. Community and technology colleges have an advantage when it comes to the opportunity to exponentially affect the student, community, business/industry, and other stakeholders through strategic partnerships.

These strategic partnerships are more than simply agreements for student job placements, training opportunities, and apprenticeships. With the appropriate competencies, data, and organizational placement, the workforce development leader's role is maximized by strategically involving themselves in the sustainability and growth of their community resulting in a multiplied impact.

Using effectual logic processes, the workforce development leader can put in place the missing competencies without having to hire additional staff and without having to learn them all themselves. This process can occur with the support of the leadership. Internal support of leadership can be garnered once certain competencies are learned by the workforce development leader and supported by community stakeholders. This is a strategy which, once put in place, becomes a roadmap to operate with less and accomplish more through strategic partnerships.

Chapter Three

Relationships Matter

Building Community Partnerships for Workforce Development

Robin Cole Jr.

"Alone we can do so little; together we can do so much."—Helen Keller

As community colleges, we have entered the twenty-first century with a renewed focus on workforce skills. The early paradigm focus was that Junior Colleges/Community Colleges were for those wanting to attend four-year institutions but needed a place to alleviate the financial burden of college while continuing their education; a structured maturation dwelling for students before making the transition to four-year colleges/universities.

The focus was developing relationships with colleges and universities and substantiating worthiness to be deemed qualified to provide transferrable academic content for higher-level institutions. Community Colleges looked to the skies above for validation concerning the education they provided. Of course, there were the technical colleges that provided job specific training, but they seemed to garner a reputation for educating those who didn't have the mental aptitude for "college."

With the focus shifting to the lack of trained professionals in technical fields, and the absence of soft skills, or as a colleague once described them, "foundational skills," among the graduates that were entering the workplace, workforce development has become a focus. The cry has beckoned out from communities, businesses, and government leaders; "institutions of higher education must develop a workforce that will replace the large number of retirees and prepare a workforce with twenty-first century skills." Therefore, with the shift in focus there is a change in the partnerships that need to be developed.

Institutions of higher education must build partnerships within the community. These partnerships include businesses, local and state government entities, employment offices, and other workforce investment agencies. Institutions of higher education naturally communicate and collaborate with each other. There is comfort partnering with those who speak a common language.

The obstacle is that, as community partnerships are built, they are often lacking in the skills and abilities to take an introduction meeting, or outreach event, and turn it into a true partnership that will support, enhance, and leverage workforce development and technical education programs. Colleges should consider a certain approach to building workforce intensive partnerships. Building these relationships takes a plan of action and rules of engagement (see figure 3.1).

RULES OF ENGAGEMENT

In the military rules of engagement are a set of rules and procedures that dictate the when, where, how, who, and which type of action should be utilized. So, think of it in this manner. The rules are set, and procedures put in place to dictate movement and actions taken. What this tells us is there is a lot of planning and thought that goes into developing these rules and procedures and each approach may not be the same, depending upon who is engaged.

The same approach can be used when looking at how to engage community and industry partnerships. "Engaging employers is an important strategy for workforce development programs; it can help align programs with employer needs so participants can secure jobs" (Barnow and Spaulding 2015; Maguire et al. 2010). Would you utilize the same approach with a Fortune 500 IT company that you would with a small architectural firm? Would you send your President to meet with local automotive technicians, or the program director of your automotive technician program? There are rules that can make engaging and building partnerships successful.

The chart below gives an example when it comes the planning of your institutions engagement. When you have a captive audience, you need to show your partners that you want a true relationship and not just a meeting. For example, this writer purposely has his first meeting with a new possible partner at their office or location. That communicates that a representative of the college is pursuing partnership in a purposeful manner. Institutions must court their partners and be in constant communication with them (see table 3.1).

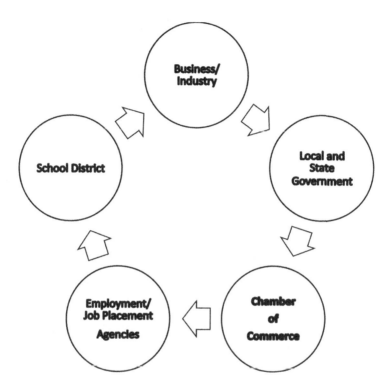

Figure 3.1. Community Partner Types. *Robin Cole Jr.*

When looking at building community partnerships engagement is necessary. *First rule of Engagement: Engagement is necessary, so be proactive.*

In a research report done for the Urban Institute, Shayne Spaulding and David Blount talked about how "workforce development programs aim to develop deeper relationships with employers that go beyond transactional job matching to become a trusted partner in realizing human resource and other related goals" (2018). Career services are a great resource when it comes to matching jobs and providing guidance for our students as they enter the workplace.

One great aspect of these services is they understand the ongoing intentional approach with helping connect the right companies with students. One key aspect of this is they take time to visit worksites and companies. The same can be said for most Workforce Development divisions within a college. Within institutions the academic affairs side of the house often only engage with partners at the advisory board meetings that sometimes occur only two to three times a year.

Table 3.1. Rules of Engagement

When	Where	Who	How	Which
Scheduled Advisory Meeting	On Campus Site	Dean, Program Coordinator, Faculty, Career Services Rep	While partners are at the meeting it is a time to not only listen to their needs, but to also give possible solutions and set up time for follow-up meeting to further enhance relationship	Is the action a lunch to just build relationship and communicate the college's resources available or is it a formal presentation of programming that can be offered?

The advisory meetings act as engagement functions when they should really be used as concentrated efforts to move initiatives, review curriculum and future training opportunities. Academic Administration and faculty should have open dialogue with community and business partners. Businesses should feel comfortable enough to reach out to you at any given time and share new developments with industry.

School Districts should be invited on a regular basis to meetings and colleges should be active in school board meetings and be seated at the table when the district is developing pipelines for K–12 students to transition into higher education. Dual Enrollment programming should be planned with the college and the school districts in constant communication and colleges need to reach out for those relationships to take place.

Attention must be paid to developing intentional relationships with community partners. Meet partners on their own turf. Never underestimate taking the time to meet partners at their place of business can be not only vital to showing a college's genuine interesting in really serving the community and providing a strong workforce, but also a chance to really see how your partner operates.

A meeting took place between a local school district, small city chamber of commerce representatives, and myself and one of my department chairs. The meeting could have taken place anywhere, but we held the meeting at the local chamber of commerce offices, within the district of the school we were meeting with. In that type of comfortable setting, the meeting turned into something that I did not expect but was vital in developing a strong partnership. The participants in the meeting began to talk about the city and its rich history, including stories about the local baseball program and how the Team USA baseball team had played there in the town.

The meeting allowed representatives of this college to see how this district and local business entities really approach partnerships as a family, and that the best approach to working with the school and the chamber was to understand that they stand united. What may sound like stories to pass time or water cooler talk, to me sounded like a group of individuals passionate about their small city and focused on its economic growth and educational pipeline into its local workforce. By coming and meeting with them on their turf it showed that the institution was genuinely interested in partnering with them and serving their community. *Second rule of engagement: Be intentional in engagement. Meet partners on their own turf.*

Katie Brown, with The National Skill Coalition, states, "Many employers do not have the capacity to consistently recruit and independently train individuals to fill jobs (2018)." This means that partnerships between community partners and community colleges allows for a constant flow of training, recruiting, and placing skilled workers into the local economy.

At Southwest Tennessee Community College, 95 percent of the graduates stay and work in the Greater Memphis, Tennessee region. This means individuals that graduate from those programs are direct contributors to the local economy and are a steady source of skilled workers for local business and industry. The community college is the pool where these companies not only fish for talent, but also restock the pool by sending their own employees to be retrained or further developed. Across the country, the need for workers is at a constant steady rate.

The companies in your region that are fixtures within the community will look to the community colleges for workers, so the engagement with them must be constant. There must be consistent dialogue and planning that involves the college, local industry, government and workforce agencies, and K–12 school districts. Building a partnership takes time, familiarity, and trust among all parties involved. *Third rule of engagement: Engagement must be consistent and ongoing.*

THE BIG FISH MENTALITY

When fishing everyone likes to catch the big fish. Those fishing competitions on television show someone hoisting in the air those massive catches. Now there are those people who fish to eat, and I have heard some fisherman say, "If it's big enough to bite its big enough to get bit back." When it comes to building partnerships Community Colleges can often find themselves wanting to build partnerships with large corporations or feel if there is not a fortune 500 company in their region then they do not have a strong workforce to support. They hear sister institutions across their state mention relationships with FedEx, Amazon, Google, and Large Universities, and they think that their partners just don't manifest the same sort of excitement or economic impact.

The U.S. Small Business Administration reports small companies accounted for 64 percent of new jobs created in the U.S. between 1993 and 2011. Small businesses represented roughly 95 percent of all U.S. companies. Those small companies and local entrepreneurs are great pipelines for students and great sources for internship opportunities for your students. New businesses accounted for virtually all-new job creation in the U.S. and nearly 20 percent of gross job creation, according to a 2015 study by the Kauffman Foundation, a research nonprofit.

In the last three decades, firms under a year old have created 1.5 million jobs annually according to the study. These numbers are stating that new partners are sprouting up all the time waiting to be engaged. Housed within Southwest Tennessee Community College we have the highest performing Small Business Development Center (SBDC) in the state of Tennessee. This organization aids entrepreneurs and new businesses in developing and equipping them with skills to further enhance their businesses.

The SBDC has a close relationship and alignment with the business department and allows students to have networking opportunities with possible employers. These small businesses also have an easy to access recruiting pool for employees as well. With evolving skills and the new generation of workers having that entrepreneurship spirit, these businesses are the new twenty-first century training and placement opportunities, but colleges must reach out and meet these new exciting partners. This means staying in constant communication with your local workforce and chamber of commerce and having a place at the table when new companies are being recruited to the area. This means being receptive to all opportunities that may be presented from various employers large and small.

Some community partnerships have a long-standing history with a college, so those partners garner the most attentions from community colleges. Those are excellent partnerships that have already been established, so don't think you will offend them by bringing new partners to the table. Those long-standing relationships should be strong enough that the partner acts as an ambassador for the college.

They should aid you in connecting with those new businesses and industry representatives as well as speak and recruit on the college's behalf. Successful community partnerships must include all organizations that support the mission of developing the local workforce within the region. The community college is that beacon in which all those entities should gather around to accomplish that goal.

ADJUNCT FACULTY:
FORGOTTEN FACES WITHIN THE COMMUNITY

As community partnerships are built, academic faculty cannot be forgotten in the equation. Dan Edmonds (2015) reported the percentage of college faculty that are part-time increased from 30 to 51 percent between 1975 and 2011. Within the technical programs at community colleges a large percentage of adjunct faculty are employed with our industry and community partners. This is an inroad advantage to building stronger community partnerships.

Community Colleges utilize community partners to help sometimes recruit highly qualified instructors for their programs. This strategy leads to buy in from partners because now they can feel confident that the instructors training the workforce will not only understand the skills they are recruiting for, but also provide them with a distinct view of the culture of those workplaces as well. Academic-community partnerships gain access to more substantial resources and more sustainable relationships if needs are connected to faculty teaching (Bloomgarden and O'Meara 2007).

When adjunct instructors from industry become a part of the faculty at the college, they also gain a greater understanding of the needs of the college, and of the full-time faculty, to better enhance the training of the students. Resources that are needed and the processes involved are now clear and the adjunct can communicate to their employer how those needs can only be met through true collaboration and industry support.

Administration may sometimes be the first level of contact when starting a partnership, but it will take buy in from faculty for it to continue to grow. Immersed adjunct faculty can be that medium for buy in on both sides of the equation. They should be immersed in their industry and immersed in the activities within the college departments as well.

DO YOU REALLY HAVE A PARTNERSHIP?

Community Colleges are presented with many opportunities for training, development, and community engagement, but sometimes it feels like an unequal commitment. Colleges sometimes feel the pressure is on them to materialize not only skilled students, but also the resources and equipment for high-level training. So, if a college feels the burden is strictly on their shoulders, do they really have a partnership? Partnerships benefit both parties. The college should feel the support of their community partners. Equipment donations, service on advisory boards/committees, even experienced instructors are ways for community partners can truly display the collaborative effort of the partnership.

Partnerships should have clear parameters set. Setting expectations as a college is reasonable. Examine if the partnership supports the mission of the college and the expectation of the educational, industry, or community partner. Building Community Partnerships are now vital for workforce development. Mona Sutphen said, "Most good relationships are built on mutual trust and respect." A community college that has truly engaged the community and has the trust and respect of its partners will be successful (see table 3.2).

TOOL BOX TO BUILD PARTNERSHIP

Mutual Interest (Foundation)

Mutual Interest is the foundation in which partnerships are built upon. "Identifying mutual benefits is the cornerstone of forming a successful partnership and guarantee to its continuity" (Sadeghnezhad 2018). The foundation must be laid before the framing of any type of partnership can be built. Mutual interest ensures cohesiveness in ideology, strategy, and plan of action when it comes to serving the community.

Strong Advisory Board Meetings (Bricks)

Strong advisory boards cannot be emphasized enough. Strong advisory boards are constantly informed, motivated to assist, and consistently present at meetings. These strengths are the bricks in the toolbox in order to support continued growth of programs and continued up-to-date reports on the business industry and changes that occur. Faculty and administrators at colleges can stay informed by reading and researching trends in the market, but those advisory members have the pertinent insight that help colleges develop programs that are ahead of the curve.

Time Spent (Nails)

Nails secure and tighten a structure. When time is spent with community partners, this secures the relationship. This secures the relationship because the community partner senses that the college genuinely values their contributions and ideas, and the college itself is consistently making itself available for the community partner to guide development of programs and trainings offered. When you think of a nail used for carpentry it has a sharp point to break through the wood. The time spent between colleges and community partners also breaks through the obstacles that can hinder beneficial community partnerships.

Table 3.2. Partnership Pathway

Partner	Avenue	Outcomes	Reasoning
Local Chamber of Commerce	College membership with the chamber of commerce	College is an active participant in workforce development updates and industry recruitment efforts by the Chamber	This leads to a clear partnership and a sign to the community and local businesses that the college has a genuine interest and investment into the local economy
Public School District/ Private Schools	Developing educational pathways through dual enrollment/dual credit	Development of a direct pipeline of students into the college.	The K–12 relationship is key for recruitment and enrollment. This also is a great way to partner on initiatives from grants to career educational exposure
	Create Summer initiatives and camps for K-12 students exposing them to educational programs and careers	Creates a clear pathway for students and school districts in order to prepare the future workforce.	
	Active recruitment efforts on and off campus in collaboration with High School Advisors	Creates a relationship with schools, students, and families within the community	
Business/ Industry Partner	Representatives from the organization are recruited to serve on the Advisory Board	College gets direct input from industry representative on needs of the organizations and changes within the specific field	In order to prepare and train students effectively the college must have a clear understanding of what the companies needs are and the skills that they consider essential for students entering the workforce

CONCLUSION

When a strong community partnership is put in place, it is a vital asset for the college and the community. The one overall factor that truly makes the effort worthwhile is the mutual benefit to both partners, the "Win-Win." Beere, Votruba, and Wells (2011) state: "Successful partnerships are mutually beneficial. The partners are unlikely to derive the same benefits, but they must derive benefits they feel are of comparable value" (203). Mutual Benefit is the paint that's added to really make all parties involved feel a sense of true completion. Mutual Benefit is appealing to all and can only be measured once all the other pieces are put in place (see figure 3.2).

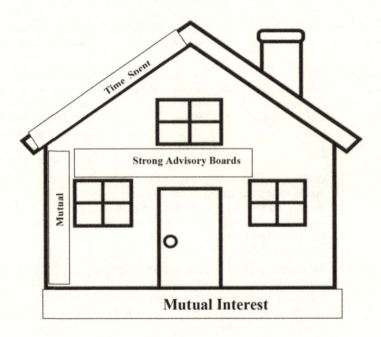

Figure 3.2.   The Foundation, Bricks, and Nails Model. *Robin Cole Jr.*

Chapter Four

Building an Agile Community College

*Strategic Transformation and
Embedding Innovation as a Competency*

Sue Ellspermann

From Michael Porter's *Competitive Forces* to Kaplan and Norton's *Balanced Scorecard* and Thomas Friedman's *The World is Flat*, we understand the importance of driving strategic change in a world of accelerating, step-function external change and expectations. Community college, long viewed as the stepchild of higher education (Obama 2009) and comfortable alternative for adults interested in continuing education, finds itself at the center of the workforce firestorm (AACC 2017).

During the Great Recession, community colleges' enrollment exploded as many states experienced double-digit unemployment and millions of Americans saw their jobs terminated, careers at a standstill, or organizations disappear. As the economy rebounded, many of these Americans returned to work, though those without college degrees and high value credentials found themselves doomed to lower pay and few options (Carnevale 2016).

Strategic planning, at its core, is simply a process for developing strategy, plans and measures which will ensure the success of the organization (Kaplan and Norton 1996). Many of these are outsourced to consulting firms tasked with developing a roadmap which will move the institution forward.

However, most often, those slick, colorful, well written plans sit on the shelf as the leaders and, more importantly, the rank and file, do not own or engage meaningfully with those plans. Further, as change accelerates, these plans become obsolete at faster rates. The nation's leading companies in the 1960s and 1970s attempted ten to twenty-five-year master plans. Today, many organizations and some experts question if two years is too long for the planning horizon.

Strategic planning is art and science. It is both process and outcome. A good strategic plan sets the mission, vision, goals, strategies, and key metrics of the organization. It may also include core values that ensure the organization maintains its True North.

Good strategic planning process understands that strategies will and must adapt to the rapid unforeseen changes in the internal and external environment. Though conditions may change, operating without a map is absurd (if you don't know where you are going, anywhere will get you there?). Is it possible to plan and continue to refine/transform that plan overtime? The author's experience suggests organizations can have both a defined strategic plan and be strategically agility. The goal is to "have your cake and eat it, too."

GENERAL READINESS FACTORS

Success in the development of a good strategic plan begins with the organization's readiness to develop a new path forward including:

- Meaningful internal and external data from which insights can be ascertained
- Willingness to share data transparently across the organization and with key external stakeholders (the good, the bad, and the ugly)
- Leaders who are prepared to change the status quo, including "breaking glass"
- Willingness of leaders to engage their teams, external stakeholders, and the entire organization in developing shared vision
- Pervasive thinking skills and culture which provides a safety environment for unpopular facts (radical candor), new ideas, and emerging strategies.
- Chief executive(s) who encourage all to engage and listen, rather than tell.
- A burning platform, that is, factors internal and/or external to the organization create heightened awareness of all associates that it cannot be "business as usual" without dire consequences such as layoffs, bankruptcy, or funding cuts.

Without most of the above factors, there is strong risk that, however polished and brilliant the strategic plan, it will be less than fully actualized.

CASE STUDY

Ivy Tech Community College is the nation's largest individually accredited and Indiana's sole community college. Ivy Tech has a budget of more than $500 million employing over 3,000 full-time employees and more than 2,000 adjunct faculty and part-time employees. Ivy Tech swelled to nearly 150,000 adult students during the Great Recession and, by 2016, had declined to nearly 100,000 students losing an average of 5 percent enrollment per year.

The good news was that Indiana's economy was rebounding faster than the national average and fastest in the Midwest as Indiana rapidly grew manufacturing jobs, as well as distribution and logistics. Simply put, adult students went back to work including thousands who went back for jobs paying less than their previous job pre-recession.

However, even with this ready workforce, all was not well with industry. As early as 2013 industry complained about the skills mismatch and inability to fill key roles such as industrial maintenance, welding, IT and nursing. During that time the Indiana Career Council, established by the Indiana General Assembly, developed a strategic plan and adopting the Lumina Goal: 60 percent of Indiana's workforce would have a post-secondary credential by 2025 (Indiana Career Council, 2014).

Becoming impatient with Ivy Tech Community College, Indiana's workforce engine, the 2016 Indiana's General Assembly mandated in statute that Ivy Tech establish a Chief Workforce Officer which would report to the President to ensure workforce alignment of programs and credentials to meet industry needs (Indiana SEA301-2016). That same year, a new president of the college was hired.

DEVELOPING A CREATIVE, INNOVATIVE CULTURE

A strategic plan is only as good as the quality of strategic thinking that underpins it. Is there an openness to data and assessment, internal and external? Is leadership able to defer judgement to hear external stakeholder feedback? To what extent are colleagues (faculty and staff) able to engage in discussions in which differing points of view are valued and leveraged? Are new ideas embraced (or killed)? To what extent is continuous improvement integrated with the day-to-day culture?

In 2016 Ivy Tech already had a robust continuous improvement environment which supported the development and use of good process. Beyond that, there was skepticism of external feedback from executive leadership and "initiative fatigue" by campus personnel as a shotgun approach to new ideas were pushed post-recession to stop the bleeding of enrollment.

SIMPLEXITY

Fall of 2016, under a new president, Ivy Tech leadership completed *Simplexity* Creative Problem Solving (Simplex). This well researched, applied method of creative problem solving is used to drive innovation in a wide range of organizations across the world (Runco 1994).

Simplex teaches four core thinking skills:

- Divergent thinking, the ability to generate many ideas, facts, challenges where novelty is encouraged
- Convergent thinking, the ability to narrow down and select best option(s) using analytical thinking and judgement
- Deferral of judgement, the ability to suspend judgement so that other ideas and points of view can be considered rather than prematurely judged
- Vertical deferral of judgement, a willingness to study an issue, define the problem prior to trying to solve the issue. Simplex prescribes an 8-step methodology for unstructured problem solving. (See figure 4.1.)

Ivy Tech's new president had 30 years of experience in various industries using, training facilitating, and consulting in Simplex. She also led strategic planning in dozens of organizations including public universities and colleges underpinned with the thinking skills and tools of Simplex. Outcomes are greatly enhanced when leaders and key participants are adept at creative thinking and trust the creative problem solving process to facilitate innovation (Basadur, 1994).

The investment in Year 1 included training all senior leaders and key middle academic, student affairs, and operations leaders in Simplex which was then used to address dozens of "fuzzy situations" to deal with significant issues, challenges and opportunities at the college. This began to create a sense of trust that those closest to the problem, using good data and insights, could identify key challenges, develop innovative solutions, and implement successful action plans. It also began creating a common language of innovation.

When we ask leaders to "lean in" to change, we must be aware that they need tools to manage and think through that change individually, in a team, and as an organization. The "How might we . . . ?" thinking of Simplex was critical to moving forward (Berger 2012).

HONESTLY ASSESS WHERE YOU ARE

In traditional strategic planning the assessment is called an environmental scan. For Ivy Tech that included Aspen Institute and Achieving the Dream

Building an Agile Community College   31

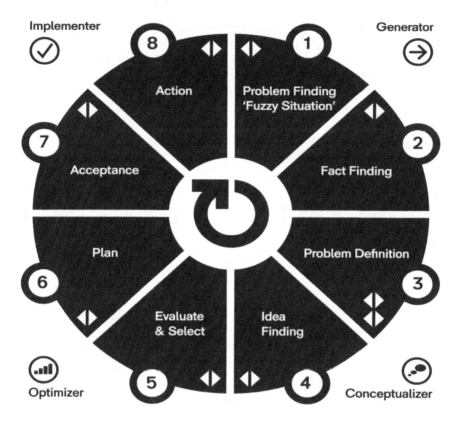

Figure 4.1. Solution Formulation. *Printed with permission from Dr. Min Basadur, Basadur Applied Creativity.*

data placing Ivy Tech performance among its peers nationally. It also engaged nearly 250 external stakeholders (industry, funders, elected leaders, industry associations, and education partners) and over 2000 faculty and staff in small group sessions to complete a Strengths Weaknesses Opportunities Threats (SWOT) analysis on Ivy Tech to gain candid feedback led by trained Simplex facilitators who modeled deferral of judgement and encouraged divergent thinking. Faculty and staff were further engaged to diverge and converge on mission and core values. This process took 6 months completing more than 50 facilitated sessions.

After this extensive input, Ivy Tech's executive leadership team and State Board of Trustees, the governing body of Ivy Tech Community College appointed by the Governor, reviewed the environmental scan, completed a SWOT Analysis, suggested core values and mission input.

CRAFT MISSION, VISION, CORE VALUE AND GOALS

During the summer of 2017 the college executive leadership team developed a "wet cement" draft of a strategic plan including: Core Values, Vision, Mission Statement, 7 Goals and emerging strategies. A team representing the President's Cabinet and Chancellors took the input from the facilitated sessions to develop institutional core values, draft mission statement (what is our purpose), vision (where do we want to go), and goals using the "How might we . . . ?" format.

The process utilized Simplex's "Why-What's Stopping Analysis" to create strategy maps for each of the goals (Ellspermann 2007). This uncovered potential key strategies and tactics. These maps serve as an illustration of the large challenge area (the goal), as well as the sub-issues and opportunities that the college might leverage as strategies. The team converged on 3–5 strategies for each goal.

"WET CEMENT"

Shared governance is core to higher education institutions. While it is impossible to have 1,500 full-time faculty members create the strategic plan; it should be a goal that all could be involved and place their "fingerprints" on the document. At Ivy Tech the president's goal was to engage in excess of 50 percent of full-time faculty members. This occurred during the assessment phase.

However, it was equally important that faculty be able to respond and refine the draft vision, mission, goals and strategies. This "wet cement version" of the strategic plan was presented to nearly 1,500 full-time faculty when they returned for Fall Semester for their feedback and support. Over 75 percent of faculty felt the emerging strategic direction was "on track" to move the college forward. Over the following semester, faculty and staff at each campus were invited to offer additional feedback and refinements. The Mission Statement and several strategies were refined as a result. Table 4.1 provides Ivy Tech's strategic plan as adopted in December 2017 by the State Board of Trustees (see textbox 4.1).

TEXTBOX 4.1. IVY TECH STRATEGIC PLAN HIGH LEVEL COMPONENTS AS ADOPTED DECEMBER 2017

Vision

Ivy Tech Community College students will earn 50,000 high-quality certifications, certificates, and degrees per year aligned with the needs of our workforce.

Mission

We are Ivy Tech, Indiana's Community College. We serve the people of our state through accessible and affordable world-class education and adaptive learning.

We empower our students to achieve their career and transfer aspirations. We embrace our vision of economic transformation inspired by the education and earnings attainment of our citizens, the vitality of our workforce, and the prosperity of our unique and diverse communities.

Core Values

Student-Centered
Outcome-Driven
Inclusive
Collaborative
Trustworthy and Transparent

Goals

Goal 1: Student Success
Goal 2: Recruitment and Enrollment
Goal 3: Completion
Goal 4: Workforce
Goal 5: Employee
Goal 6: Financial
Goal 7: Community

Source: Developing "Metrics that Matter"

Once goals are established, meaningful metrics must follow to gauge progress. Higher education has its own cadre: enrollment, persistence rates, on-time completion, equity and many more. The statement, "What gets measured, get done" is generally held as a truth. Identifying metrics (key performance indicators) which measure progress to a goal do not always exist. This process took more than a year to develop metrics in areas such as workforce alignment ensuring programs matched employer needs and gaining actual wage data of recent graduates. For Goal 5, Being a Great Place to Work, Ivy Tech worked with a third party to measure employee engagement.

For Goal 7, "Putting more community in community college," Ivy Tech worked with another firm to develop a community engagement survey completed by community leaders annually. Performance expectations were set to be "challenging, but realistic" based on external stakeholder needs and top quartile high performing community colleges. This led to significant stretch including growing enrollment 3 percent per year . . . even while most community colleges continue to shrink.

Year over year completions need to increase more than 10 percent each year to go from 20,000 to 50,000 over 5 years. The performance measures are forcing the college out of complacency to boldly pursue new methods and ideas. These measures remain visible, are integrated into campus reviews, performance reviews, and reported on in every State Board meeting and with the legislature. Textbox 4.2 provides a summary of Ivy Tech metrics.

TEXTBOX 4.2. IVY TECH METRICS ALIGNED TO GOALS OF THE STRATEGIC PLAN

		Year 1	Year 3	Year 5
Goal 1:	Fall to Spring Retention	70%	75%	80%
	Fall to Fall Retention	50%	55%	60%
Goal 2:	Revenue Headcount	100,472	107,625	119,787
	Recruit Headcount	50,598	52,901	56,122
Goal 3:	Total Credentials	23,000	30,000	50,000
	Completing in 100% Time	8%	14%	22%
	Completing in 150% Time	15.8%	22.4%	30%
	Completing in 300% Time	18.8%	26.4%	35%
Goal 4:	Percent Completions in High Demand/Low Supply Programs	70%	40%	10%
	Percent Completions in High Demand/Limited Enrollment Programs	12.5%	10.5%	5%

		Year 1	Year 3	Year 5
	Percent Completions in Low Demand/High Supply Programs	7.5%	6.5%	5%
	Percent Completions in Demand/Supply Equilibrium	10%	43%	80%
	Percent graduates above Median Wages Within 1 year of graduation	41%	53%	80%
Goal 5:	College Employee Engagement Survey Score	72 out of 100	74 out of 100	76 out of 100
Goal 6:	Reserves Days on Hand	180 days	180 days	180 days
	Reserves Percent Annual Growth	3%	3%	3%
	Total Foundation Dollars Raised	52.3M	$64.6M	$64.2M
Goal 7:	Community Satisfaction Survey	8+ out of 10	8+ out of 10	8+ out of 10

AFFIRMATION AND ROLL OUT

In December 2017 the State Board of Trustees adopted Ivy Tech's new strategic plan, "Our Communities. Your College: Pathways for Student Success and a Stronger Indiana." In January the plan was shared with the Governor, Indiana's Commission for Higher Education, legislators, industry associations, economic development, higher education, and philanthropic partners. The president and senior executives presented dozens of times across the state over the following year. The full strategic plan can be found on Ivy Tech's website (Ivy Tech 2019).

THE FIRST YEAR

All current college structures required adjusting: curriculum committees, student success priorities, performance reviews and incentive plans, campus review process, capital allocation, and budgeting. The first year of a plan is most critical. It must be intentional and show success. The VP of Strategic Planning and Change Management set up a structure including:

- *Goal Sponsors*: 1 Cabinet executive + 1 Campus chancellor.
- *Strategy Owners*: 1 Systems Office leader + 1 campus leader. Selected for their expertise and ownership of key functions relating to the strategy.

- *Strategy Team Members*: Functional stakeholders and volunteers from across the college with interest in moving the strategy forward.
- *Strategic Rotation Leads*: A six-month professional development position where an administrator, faculty or staff member spends 10-20 percent of their time serving as facilitator to a Goal to ensure progress towards the strategies with specific tactics and implementation plans.

Goal sponsors, strategy owners and strategic rotation leads were gathered to kick-off in early February to establish expectations. Each month Strategic Rotation Leads host a Goal Call where Strategy Owners report on progress. Monthly a report is developed which the President and Cabinet members receive. At six months, the first Strategic Plan Update brought together Goal Sponsors, Cabinet and Chancellors to review early progress and refinements to plans.

ANNUAL STRATEGIC PLAN REFRESH

At the one year mark all metrics were moving in the right direction with one significant laggard, Recruitment and Enrollment, Goal 2. Thus, the goal underwent a significant refresh embedding year 1 learnings and developing much stronger strategies. At the year 1 refresh session a second occurrence was unexpected. While the college had tried to embed diversity, inclusion and reduction of equity gaps, it was realized after the first year that, without a goal, specific strategies, and metrics, the college was not making sufficient progress.

College leaders made the recommendation to add Goal 8: Diversity, Equity and Belonging. This initiated a planning process for a new goal and has been met with strong support by the State Board, external stakeholders, and, most importantly, faculty, staff and students. To date, more than 200 faculty, staff and students have participated in facilitated sessions to refine and map this goal. Metrics are under development.

One could say, doesn't this show how imperfect the initial plan was? You could. Or, you could see how the refresh process, the new goal and several strategy adjustments re-energized the plan laser-focused on progress that matters to students, employers and the State of Indiana.

CELEBRATING EARLY WINS

After 18 months, all campuses, all departments, and the majority of faculty and staff are "rowing in the same direction" as it is now crystal clear what the priorities of the institution are aligned to ensuring each student succeeds, more students are enrolled, and students complete 50,000 high wage, high value credentials per year aligned to workforce needs. Ten of twelve metrics were met the first year. Only one campus met all their metrics in the first year. However, all are showing signs of improvement and several are "within a stone's throw" of reaching all metrics.

WHEN IS IT TIME FOR A NEW PLAN?

At the time of publication, the college was approaching the end of its second year. An annual refresh will be completed each year. A construct is being developed to assess when it will be time to "reinvent" the plan. Several indicators a new plan should be developed include:

- A new president from outside the college who brings a new direction.
- A major external occurrence such as state funding being slashed, new responsibilities given to the college from the legislature, or a major technological innovation which quickly changes the education landscape.
- Changing expectations of students or employers which might require the college to greatly alter services.
- Significant over or underperformance to the plan which suggests the current goals and strategies are "off the mark."
- The plan is no longer "living and breathing", that is, there is no longer accountability tied to it.

The author finds that the latter is the most common, followed by new leadership and external forces that render the current plan insufficient for the world.

CONCLUSION

One cannot overstate the important role leaders play in the success of strategic planning. The chief executive must be present, listen, engage, and champion the process and outcomes of the plan. S/he must "own the plan" including placing to memory each goal, strategy, and metric. S/he should take every opportunity to link initiatives and successes to the strategic plan. S/he must elevate that plan both internally and externally. And, s/he should use failure to meet metrics to create a burning platform under goals which are more difficult, under sourced, or lack commitment.

At Ivy Tech, Goal 2, Recruitment and Enrollment, is our most significant challenge as is experienced nationally as community colleges continue to lose enrollment in a full employment economy. That would be acceptable for Ivy Tech if we were achieving the state's goal for educational attainment, employers' had the credentialed employees they needed, and/or all Hoosiers were enjoyed at or above the nation's median wage. In fact, none of those are true. Thus, though we have not met our performance metric, we have begun to grow and have undertaken strategic enrollment management combining very intentional high school and adult strategies with numerous external stakeholders.

And, while leadership is critical, process leadership is equally important. The chief executive cannot manage the day-to-day of the strategic plan implementation. It takes a masterful general to organize these activities. A process-oriented chief strategy officer ensures the "machine is working", real progress is being made, and makes real-time adjustments to those engaged with specific goals and strategies. The chief strategy officer is the chief executive's "right hand" in this work.

At the end of the day, the goal is to create an agile organization which understands that change is continuous and "leans in" to external and internal forces of change with new and evolving solutions. This actualizes what Henry Mintzberg, twice awarded Harvard Business School's McKinsey Award for best Harvard Business Review article, called "crafting strategy" (Mintzberg 1987). Mintzberg summarizes crafting strategy as

- managing stability
- detecting discontinuity
- knowing the business
- managing patterns, and
- reconciling change and continuity.

Community colleges and education, in general, need to learn to continuously improve our core competencies of student learning and credential completion, while building new competencies such as recruitment, student support services, career development and placement, new credentialing types, and learning modalities based on transformational changes occurring in the workforce as a result of technology, global forces, and demographic shifts already underway ensuring the future of work will look very different than it does today.

To power a thriving American economy, a growing middle class, and to remain relevant, community colleges must boldly lead higher education transformation. Effective strategic planning processes can help create the agile community colleges American industry needs and America's current and future workforce deserves.

REFERENCES

American Association of Community Colleges. 2017. "Community Colleges: Addressing the Skills Gap." https://www.aacc.nche.edu/wp-content/uploads/2017/10/SkillsGapReport

forPrint.pdf.

Basadur, Min. 1994. "Managing the Creative Process in Organizations" In *Problem Finding Problem Solving and Creativity,* edited by Mark Runco, 253-268. Norwood, New Jersey: Greenwood Publishing Group.

Berger, Warren. "The Secret Phrase Top Innovators Use." *Harvard Business Review,* September 17, 2012.

Carnevale, Anthony, Tamara Jayasundara, and Artem Gulish. 2016. "America's Divided Recovery: College Haves and Have-Nots," Georgetown University Center on Education and the Workforce report. https://1gyhoq479ufd3yna29x7ubjn-wpengine.netdna-ssl.com/wp-content/uploads/Americas-Divided-Recovery-web.pdf.

Ellspermann, Susan, Gerald Evans, and Min Basadur. 2007. "The Impact of Training on the Formulation of Ill-structured Problems." *Omega: The International Journal of Management Science* 35, no. 2.

Friedman, Thomas. 2005. *The World is Flat: A Brief History of the Twenty-first Century.* New York: Farrar, Straus, and Giroux.

Indiana Career Council. 2014. "Align, Engage, Advance: A Strategic Plan to Transform Indiana's Workforce", https://businessengagement.workforcegps.org/-/media/Communities/rapidresponse/Files/Sector-Strategies/Skill_Building_Resources/Indiana_Career_Council_Strategic_Plan_-_Align_Engage_Advance_-_FINAL.ashx

Indiana Senate Enrolled Act 301, 2016. http://iga.in.gov/legislative/2016/bills/senate/301#document-ab72be4d.

Ivy Tech Community College. 2019. "Ivy Tech Strategic Plan." https://strategicplan.ivytech.edu/.

Kaplan, Robert, and Norton, David. 1996. *The Balanced Scorecard.* Boston: Harvard Business School Press.

Mintzberg, Henry. 1987. "Crafting Strategy" In *Strategy: Seeking and Securing Competitive Advantage,* edited by Cynthia Montgomery and Michael Porter, 403–20. Boston: Harvard Business School Press.

Obama, Barack. 2009. "Remarks at Macomb Community College," Speech by President Obama, July 14, 2009.

Porter, Michael. 1991. "How Competitive Forces Shape Strategy" In *Strategy: Seeking and Securing Competitive Advantage,* edited by Cynthia Montgomery and Michael Porter, 11–25. Boston: Harvard Business School Press.

Chapter Five

Rising with the Machines

Embracing Opportunity—and Living Your Values—in an Age of Transformation

Lee D. Lambert

Given that in the past few years, machines have performed surgery, picked stock investments, delivered groceries, operated high-speed rail, conducted legal research, diagnosed diseases, and maybe most important, started to talk back, it's safe to say we are living in a new era. The world is entering a Fourth Industrial Revolution, an economic upheaval triggered by rapid technological advances such as mobile technology, artificial intelligence, cloud-based computing and the Internet of Things.

It would not be a stretch to think of these forces as "superpowers," because, in the words of Pat Gelsinger, Chief Executive Officer of VMWare, a global firm specializing in digital infrastructure, they are on a par with "major nations, shaping the course of history."

History is rife with examples of technological disruptions upending the employment landscape. The perils of the current tectonic shifts are evident from a quick scan of the daily headlines on one's Internet-connected mobile device. Approximately 50 percent of current work activities are automatable by adapting currently demonstrated technologies, according to the research firm McKinsey. The World Economic Forum estimates that 65 percent of today's first graders will work in jobs that do not currently exist. By 2020, Gartner Inc. forecasts that artificial intelligence will create 2.3 million jobs worldwide while eliminating 1.8 million. (An aside to those reading this from the safety of the executive suite: McKinsey estimates that 20 percent of all duties currently performed by CEOs can be automated using today's technology. In other words, do not get too comfortable.)

Moreover, higher education faces challenges that have little to do with technology. It has been well-documented that the number of births in the U.S. has declined since the Great Recession of 2008. This "birth dearth" will cause stark challenges for workforce development and college enrollment due to population stagnation.

We also live in an era of increased competition. The plethora of online education opportunities available to students means that a college's brick-and-mortar and online programs are competing against programs stood up by the private sector in our city, as well as programs thousands of miles away.

Federal government and accreditor scrutiny of higher education also has increased. More and more, accreditors are focused on outcomes, in the form of proof of student learning, or data regarding employment of graduates. Pima recently hosted a comprehensive evaluation visit from its accreditor, the Higher Learning Commission, and is working tirelessly to satisfy the HLC's monitoring requirements and to continue our improvement plan. The HLC's next visit is in 2024. For Pima and higher education, accreditation is a fact of life.

For community college and other higher education CEOs, the question is how to manage and leverage the coming transformation of the economy for the benefit of their students, institutions and communities. Northeastern University President Dr. Joseph Aoun, in his book *Robot-Proof*, succinctly outlines the challenge and opportunity: "To stay relevant in this new economic reality, higher education needs a dramatic realignment. Instead of educating college students for jobs that are about to disappear under the rising tide of technology, twenty-first-century universities should liberate them from outdated career models and give them ownership of their own futures."

Dr. Aoun's charge to liberate students means higher education leaders must make foundational changes to their institution, while ensuring their schools remain true to their mission and core beliefs. Pima Community College's approach to tackling that formidable task, especially as it connects with workforce development, constitutes the remainder of this chapter. In the past five years, Pima has strategically embraced opportunities to be the provider of educational content for Career and Technical Education students, employers and incumbent workers in our region.

We are animated by the words of Anthony Carnevale, director and research professor of Georgetown University's Center on Education and Workforce, who has written, "What you earn depends much more on what you take in college than where you go. "From a career perspective, college is more a market in program majors than a market in institutions."

Prefaced by the caveat that no one-size-fits-all solution exists, our initiatives have yielded insights and lessons worth presenting to our colleagues in the spirit of collaboration and shared mutual interest.

LESSONS WORTH LEARNING: A CHECKLIST

Dig into the Data

Pima research has uncovered a noticeable gap between the median age of our enrollees in Applied Technology programs and enrollees in transfer-oriented programs. The median age of enrollees in programs such as mathematics, communications, sciences, and developmental education hovers around 19-20 years, while the median age of those enrolled in CTE areas such as Applied Technology, Allied Health, and Nursing programs is 28-30 years.

Pima is operating under the assumption that, upon high school graduation, many graduates enter lower-skilled jobs and meander through the labor market for about a decade—Pima has labeled it "the lost decade"—before enrolling in Pima's Applied Technology programs with the intention of pursuing programs of study that lead to higher wages and gainful employment.

Armed with this knowledge, Pima is shaping its programs to meet the unique needs of the demographic. We are committed to offering multiple on-ramps to education, such as stackable certificates; short-term, industry-driven training opportunities; programs that can be completed entirely online; and giving credit for prior learning.

For example, Pima is standing up a tuition reimbursement program with national insurance provider GEICO's expanding Tucson operation. To serve GEICO employees, Pima will offer wraparound student services as well as a variety of modalities—classes may be taken online, at GEICO facilities, or on our campuses. GEICO receives real-time information on its students' progress so that it can monitor the benefits of the investment. Everyone wins.

Know Your Neighborhood

Despite the stateless nature of technological change, it is still important to develop situational awareness. Pima is located in Tucson, Arizona. Interstate 10 runs through Tucson and Phoenix to Los Angeles. The Tucson-Phoenix I-10 corridor is home to new manufacturing operations of some of America's biggest corporations, such as Raytheon Missile Systems, Boeing Co. and Intel Corp. We are well aware of the opportunity Pima has to be a key player in the economic development of our transnational region if we work with regional business and education partners.

One promising partnership is the one-of-a-kind Arizona Advanced Technology Network (AATN) project spearheaded by Pima, Maricopa Community Colleges in Phoenix, and Central Arizona College in Coolidge, located at the midpoint between the two larger cities. The AATN offers a common technology curriculum approved by industries along the corridor. Moreover, each college will offer courses specializing in teaching skills that are needed by its neighboring business. In the same vein, Pima, cognizant that some 8,000 cybersecurity jobs are unfilled in Arizona, will offer a degree in Cybersecurity in Fall 2019. We recently partnered with the Arizona Cyber Warfare Range and are the only community college in the United States to offer "live-fire" (real-world) cyber-scenarios.

Understand the role your institution plays in the economic development of your region. Pima occupies a unique position in the "human capital" pipeline. Pima works with business and industry, K-12 and the state's three public universities, including the University of Arizona in Tucson, to ensure that Southern Arizona has a pool of talented, work-ready employees, so that existing businesses can expand and new businesses can relocate.

Distinguish the short term versus the long term. Community colleges intent on improving their standing in the workforce development space must recognize the need to meet employer expectations in the short term while simultaneously preparing for business and industry needs of the future. A case in point is truck driver training. It is well known that the trucking industry is facing a shortage of qualified drivers, and Pima's Truck Driver Training program delivers a comprehensive curriculum designed to quickly put highly qualified drivers on the road.

It should be well-known that automation threatens to put many of these truckers out of a job. Walmart, for example, has begun testing driverless trucks to ferry groceries through west Phoenix. To prepare truckers for the future, Pima has partnered with TuSimple, a San Diego-based autonomous vehicle manufacturer with facilities in Tucson. TuSimple foresees the need for twenty-first-century truckers to possess a special set of skills: interacting with the truck's computer systems, tracking cargo as it progresses through the supply chain, occasionally taking the wheel, and repairing the truck when it breaks down. Our faculty, staff and administrators are working with TuSimple to design a Pima truck driver training program in which technologies as diverse as optics, information technology and logistics will converge in the trucker's cab. Launched in June, this certificate program, Autonomous Vehicle Driver & Operations Specialist, appears to be the first of its kind in the United States.

Heal thyself. Break down internal institutional silos that often result in units of the college working inefficiently or at cross-purposes. Keep everyone focused on the college's mission. Flatten your organization. Embrace "management by walking around." Provide the community one point of contact for workforce and economic development. At Pima, the Office of Workforce Development, led by a Vice President, is the clearinghouse for all workforce and economic development initiatives.

Embrace the importance of professional relationships. Community college CEOs must engage their C-level counterparts in the government, education, industry, and community sectors. Make it an expectation that College administrators will establish and expand their professional networks in order to reap the benefits of increased engagement. A professional relationship between Pima's Vice President of Workforce Development and the Director of Research at the Center for International Trade & Transportation in Long Beach, Calif., eventually led to Pima's inclusion in the Pacific Southwest Region (PSR) University Transportation Center (UTC) partnership.

The partnership is helping drive advances in our Logistics and Supply Chain Management and Truck Driver Training programs. Pima is one of the first community colleges to become part of a UTC. The collaboration is central to our empowerment of the new mobility workforce. At its core, the PSR UTC project epitomizes adaptability and convergence, two elements that are common to many emerging technologies. Among the key initiatives Pima is working on are integrating Geospatial Information System (GIS) technology into Logistics and Truck Driver Training; integrating employability or "soft skills" into these new models; and delivering education to underserved and rural populations, with an emphasis on tribal populations in the American Southwest.

Understand the interplay between old and new. It is critical to provide curriculum that only serves the immediate needs of employers but also provides students with portable skills that will be valuable wherever they work. One of the best elements of the Arizona Advanced Technology Network is offering the Arizona Career Readiness Credential, which helps ensure core work-readiness. The ACRC measures skills in professionalism, teamwork, critical thinking, communication, applied math, reading, and workforce data and graphics. In the twenty-first century, these competencies will be in demand wherever an employee works.

Collaborate, collaborate, collaborate. It should be obvious from these cases-in-point that, in an era of decreasing public funding, higher education institutions cannot go it alone. We need public-private partnerships. Pima recently connected with global heavy-equipment manufacturer Caterpillar Inc. to create the Applied Technology Academy at Pima. The Academy offers a series of hands-on courses designed to teach fabrication skills to engineers and other non-technical professionals. Engineers do not always have hands-on or end-user experience with products they design. The Academy will deepen their understanding of how product design impacts quality, manufacturability, field serviceability and customer value downstream.

RETOOLING YOUR WORKFORCE FOR THE FUTURE

The initiatives described above are heartening, as they indicate Pima is making innovative, proactive change at a high level. But the reality is that the College is not immune to the same emerging pressures impacting workforces across the nation and globe. As McKinsey and Co. note, companies designing their workforce of the future face a variety of challenges if they are to succeed in a world prizing higher cognitive, social, and technological skills over basic cognitive and manual skills.

In the footsteps of McKinsey, Pima has devised a plan that combines retraining employees by teaching them new skills, redeploying employees by redefining work tasks, realizing the potential of the gig economy and an expanding contract-worker pool, and, as painful as it is, releasing workers, usually by attrition and retirement but sometimes through layoffs. Responding to acute financial pressures common among community colleges (declining enrollment) and specific to Arizona (a state-mandated expenditure limitation), the College has embarked on a successful budget-reduction strategy that unfortunately has included a few involuntary separations from compensation.

With that necessary period of correction behind us, the College, through its Human Resources unit, is focusing its attention on talent acquisition. We are intent on building talent communities -- identifying through personal and professional relationships candidates for future jobs, and regularly touching base with them through informational emails about College activities. This is an essential element for any organization wishing to keep itself top-of-mind. We hire for attitude, which is innate, as much as aptitude, which can be taught. We are aware of next-generation HR tools that can help us automate initial evaluations of a large number of résumés, while being cognizant that a human touch is a necessary element of any substantive decision.

POLICY VS. CULTURE AND THE POWER OF EMPOWERMENT

The goal for any healthy organization is for its policies to be indistinguishable from its culture. To define "culture" I will rely on the elegantly succinct definition put forth by organizational management scholars Allan Kennedy and Terrence Deal nearly 40 years ago: "The way things are done around here." Culture bubbles up from myriad daily incremental actions conducted by employees interacting with each other, in the most granular way. It isn't found in collections of administrative procedures, or in handbooks. If you are not witnessing it on the ground, it is difficult to recognize. Yet culture is real, and the extent that policy and culture diverge is a challenge for the organization.

By observing a unique culture such as the U.S. Army, there are lessons higher education administrators can learn from the military, an entity that is wildly different from academia. Let's begin with this question: How do our nation's armed forces take wildly diverse recruits, many of whom are teens, and in a few years transform them into focused soldiers given huge tactical, strategic, and potentially life-and-death responsibilities affecting their units and the greater collective effort? The answers are many, but higher education CEOs should recognize the key concept, as it is one they often invoke: empowerment.

It is important to know what empowerment is not. Empowerment does not entail merely delegating responsibility to subordinates. The most effective organizations do not just download authority to accomplish tasks according to a pre-determined procedure; they empower subordinates to accomplish those tasks as they see best. Empowerment is based on the understanding that employees on the ground often are the best-equipped to diagnose problems, devise solutions, and to suggest innovations. The benefits of the empowerment approach are many. An empowered workforce takes ownership of its tasks, thinks critically, obtains more satisfaction from the job and is more productive. Though extremely hierarchical, the military loosens control by handing its employees the car keys, as it were. The question for higher education CEOs is if they are willing to do the same.

CONCLUSION

Any CEO should be exhilarated by, if a little apprehensive of, the opportunities rising to the surface in this new era. The years ahead offer the possibility of carving out pre-eminent positions in new sectors—the opportunity to be first-to-market, to be No. 1 in a category—while surmounting revenue and enrollment challenges. But chancellors and presidents of public higher education institutions are not any CEOs. They sit atop tax-and-tuition funded schools, not businesses. They have shareholders, not stockholders. Increasing revenue is not their sole motive. Their performances will be scored not only against a balance sheet, but against the upholding of the core values of their institutions.

Pima Community College has embarked on many new initiatives in the past five years. Underlying all of them is a steadfast commitment to our tripartite institutional North Star of student success, community engagement and diversity, as well as the principle of open access. Our values meld well with our community. Tucson is a wonderfully multicultural city that, unfortunately, also is one of the most impoverished communities of its size in the U.S., and among the most economically stratified. Thousands of Tucsonans need Pima to climb that critical first rung on the ladder of economic prosperity. By necessity Pima is an instrument of economic, and hence social, equity.

The new era of technology offers Pima and similar institutions an opportunity to level the playing field for historically marginalized populations. But the College must understand these inequities, and be strategic and holistic in its approaches. We must acknowledge the structural inequities of the past, some of which have been decades or even centuries in the making. Pima cannot merely present information about promising new programs to everyone. We must do more than build it and hope they will come, because history has shown that high-income students are better situated to reap the benefits of higher education than are their lower-income counterparts. As the Brookings Institution states in a 2018 report, "policies designed to help students prepare for the future workforce that fail to account for existing inequalities will likely perpetuate these inequalities."

That is why our aforementioned partnership with the University Transportation Center included an initiative to aid indigenous populations. It's why Pima's integrated planning calls for enhanced outreach to the underserved, across the board, and why our marketing efforts target underserved audiences. That is why our initiative with Caterpillar is part of a larger plan to build a Center of Excellence in Applied Technology on a campus in a gritty, up-and-coming neighborhood, and why, in conjunction with urban development partners, we are exploring collaborations to bring a community healthcare clinic, neighborhood center and small-format food retail to the Center.

The new era promises to deliver amazing new technology; however, technology is but a means to a greater end. Pima's aspirational goal is to wield technology to ameliorate inequity. It is not the easiest approach. But it is crucial to our communities.

And it is worth repeating: *Do not get too comfortable.*

Part II

Internal Issues Affecting Community College Workforce Development

Chapter Six

Making a Case for Workforce Development

Ty A. Stone

UNDERSTANDING THE ENVIRONMENT

In the role of a new President, the very first action taken was to learn as much of the culture and environment of the college. This worked in two ways: one, to make certain that the college had the ability to and acceptance of organizational change, and two, to gather the real needs of the community the college serves.

Before arriving at the new institution, the strategic approach decided upon would be to engage the executive staff and board to create a list of key community influencers that would be receptive to hearing from the new President upon her arrival. The goal was to learn as much about the climate and the needs of the community as quickly as possible. The plan for the first 100 days, was to conduct forums on campus, and to invite students, faculty, and staff. It was also imperative to schedule meetings with a variety of stakeholders in the community—county legislators, superintendents, military leaders, and key employers. All meetings were structured around three key questions that hopefully would provide an understanding of the climate and the foundation for the future direction that the college should be taking.

These questions are not earth-shattering or groundbreaking. These were questions that we, as administrators used at my last college when we were assessing the state of the departments we were tasked with overseeing. The three questions are:

1. What do we do well?
2. What needs attention?

3. What would you advise me to prioritize in a plan and why?

DOCUMENTING THE PROCESS

Copious notes were taken from the various meetings, and then a team distilled the data collected to identify themes in their responses. This activity helped to gain a greater understanding of the need in this community. These questions were used to guide the fact-finding mission, most of what was documented provided the foundation necessary to move forward with workforce training as a priority. The college had enjoyed decades of success as a traditional, liberal arts transfer institution. Our completion rates, while not where we wanted them to be, are still quite respectable on the national scene. However, as with other colleges, the college was in a position that change had to happen. Enrollment has been declining for over five years, and there appeared to be a misalignment between what industry told us they needed and what the newly minted college graduates were bringing with them in the way of skills and abilities.

Further, the community overwhelmingly shared with us their need to source, train, attract, and retain people with skills, and that their dependence on degrees as the bellwether to prove that graduates possessed adequate skills was no longer serving them well. They implored that they needed people who could *do* the job—and that the degree did not matter.

Managing Change

For many at the college, change is a daunting process. Not unlike many of our long-standing institutions across the country, our staff have long memories. We were often faced with discussions that ended in "we tried that 20 years ago, and it didn't work." However, as we continue to talk, many understand the need to take risks and to be true to our mission, which is to quickly respond to the unique needs of our community. We were also faced with the fear from many that we would abandon the past work that we have done so well to shift to workforce training. The President assured them over the first two years that the process of building strong workforce training programs does not take away from the core work we have done over the decades, which is providing two-year degrees and transfer opportunities for four-year degrees for our students. The workforce training program is not an "or," it is an "and." We will create workforce training programs AND provide opportunities to pursue degrees for our students.

Building Trust

As a new president, in a new community, with a new agenda, it is critical to gain trust very early on. Gaining this trust is not a quick process. As a matter of fact, it takes a long time to gain trust—and even longer to keep trust. In addition to trust, the leader must find a coalition of faculty and staff that are believers in the new direction.

A new leader must embody the character and behavior the community wishes to see, and the new President must work hard to do just that. That means listening to the opinions of others, even when pressed for time; it means taking time to connect with students, faculty, and staff across the organization, even when other things that must be done.

Making the case for workforce development is becoming less and less difficult, as most understand that this is the national trend for community colleges. Our towns and cities are struggling with the crushing reality of the middle skills gap, and this is precisely the work that community colleges do well. Employers are finding it more difficult than ever to find people with the right skills to do the jobs that need to be done. Nevertheless, for many community colleges, moving in that direction is a shift in how they've operated in the "degrees for everyone" era.

DATA MATTERS

As you are making the case for workforce development, it is critically important to provide data that supports the shift to this new agenda, which should not be too difficult to find. Data points that include the key industries in your area, the job projections, the average wages, are all important to ensure that the organization's leaders are focusing on the right kinds of training to fill the demands of the area. For our region, those were advanced manufacturing and construction. Meetings were held with individuals from several organizations in these fields, and they all said the same thing—they needed more people with the skills to do the work. Many of them were worried because they were not able to pursue contracts because of the lack of qualified people to carry out the work. As we further explored ways to deliver a solution to the needs of our community, the President and her staff hosted industry roundtable conversations. At these meetings, specific industry leaders from across the region came together to discuss the challenges they face related to the workforce. The first industry we met with was the construction industry. Leaders from union and non-union organizations had the same issues—they sat at the same table to work toward solutions to a central problem. Our staff documented their needs and we followed up with them to make certain that we interpreted their needs appropriately.

ENSURING BUY-IN

Documentation of the themes from these types of meetings is very important to ensure that the college community understands the significance of this issue. We held numerous meetings with a variety of stakeholders across the college to share the information that we had received. Many in higher education, especially those long-term employees, have experienced "change fatigue," and it is understandable. We have, through the years, asked them to adjust, change, revamp their practices to address some emerging trend. However, this is different. The information and data illustrate just how serious the middle skills gap is. We don't believe that this will be a passing fancy, but, instead, will be the differentiating factor between those institutions that provide workforce training well, and those that do not. For this initiative, we feel very strongly that historical community colleges were established for this, and therefore, we are now going back to our roots.

It is also critically important to bring the board along as you move toward this new way of operating. On our board were members who had served as long as some of my long-term staff. They have also seen the multiple changes and initiatives that have been proposed over the years and are sensitive to how these changes can affect students, staff, and the budget. In a time when enrollment is down and funding is also diminishing, it is important to demonstrate that workforce training is an investment that involves great risk, but also great reward. In addition to the board, if you have a foundation, they should also be advised of the great need for skills-based training. We have begun to work with our donors (both current and prospective) to establish scholarships to assist for the tuition for our non-credit training.

Also, the challenge of funding must be addressed. Currently, there are no federal or state financial aid funds to pay for non-credit, short-term training programs. Our institution has been successful in receiving grants to help us create these programs and to offer them to cohorts, but the funding is not sustained. Further, it is cost prohibitive for many un- and under-employed to privately pay for these types of training. We have been very vocal at the local, state and national levels of our need to identify funding to help pay for training for people. Whether it is education or training, we should find opportunities to help people get the skills they need to do the work that needs to be done in our communities.

CONCLUSION

Within the first year, the President was successful in demonstrating to the college community, local sponsor, and the community at large the importance of investing in workforce training programs. We were successful in attaining financial support from our adjacent county to build a building that supports training for the community. We partnered with the local career technical school to create alignment for a training pipeline that starts in high school. In the six months it has been opened, we have trained hundreds of individuals, and completed a cohort of 30 construction trainees with a national certification. Every one of those in the construction trades program was employed within a month of their completion. As we reflect on that statistic, it is incredibly rewarding to know that our willingness to partner and take risks has perhaps changed the trajectory of the lives of dozens and will continue to do so for many more to come.

Chapter Seven

Understanding Equity and its Importance in Developing the Workforce of the Future

Angela Davis, Susan Paris, and Jairo McMican

Community colleges are at the center of every issue of workforce and economic development affecting our state. Dallas Herring, a visionary of the NC Community College System, believed that community colleges should meet all students where they are, maintain an open-door philosophy, and create pathways to help them achieve success. In order to embrace all students, community colleges and industry partners must develop strategies that produce equitable outcomes for all students.

Over the past ten years, Durham Technical Community College and Central Carolina Community College have embarked on a journey to develop an equity-mindset, in an effort to help all students achieve their desired goals. Community, business and industry and public-school collaboration has been a key factor in this effort. We offer the following tools for understanding equity will better inform all stakeholders on ways to close equity gaps and develop the diverse workforce of the future.

DIVERSITY, EQUITY, AND INCLUSION: WHAT'S THE DIFFERENCE?

Diversity, inclusion and equity are common terms used across all industries. Defining the terms effectively and creating a culture where equity becomes a mindset has proven to be a difficult task for many leaders. Diversity can be described as embracing the unique differences of others. These differences include people who belong to groups that are protected by law. These may include people of a particular race, religion, color, national origin, sex and people with disabilities.

A diverse workforce fosters creativity and helps any organization achieve its full potential. An organization that values diversity may implement strategies to ensure the recruitment and retention of diverse candidates. Vernā Myers, Vice President of Inclusion Strategy at Netflix, describes diversity as an invitation to the dance. Others have described diversity as having a seat at the table.

Inclusion promotes a culture where people feel valued, accepted and respected. Inclusivity helps to create openness in the workplace and fosters an environment of trust. An inclusive work environment ensures that everyone has equal access to services and resources. An employer that promotes an inclusive work environment has employees who are engaged and feel supported at work. Now that an employee has been invited to the dance, Vernā Myers describes inclusion as being about asking individuals to dance, which is reflective of the concept of diversity. Inclusion provides the employees sitting at the table with an invitation to speak and have a voice.

Equity in the workplace is a harder concept to understand. Organizations can impact diversity by implementing new recruitment and retention strategies which is important, but this is not what equity means. Similarly plans of inclusion may involve the creation of a diversity and inclusion council that provides a safe place for employees to voice concerns, while ensuring that everyone's voice is heard, but this is also not what equity means. Changing organizational or systemic practices, policies or procedures, which is central to equity, is much more difficult to define and implement.

Equity is intentional, and not only ensures that people have equitable access to resources, but removes institutional barriers that make it difficult to access those resources. Equity acknowledges that some people have power that provides them various advantages while others do not have access to the same power structure. For example, if a company says they promote professional development and growth for all employees, but requires their employees to pay for travel and registration costs upfront and wait for reimbursement, entry-level employees are less likely to be able to participate in professional growth opportunities.

Achieving equity is essential to ensure that all underrepresented students have the same opportunities for access and completion in education and in the workplace as students who have resources and privileges that make their attendance and completion of college more predictable and attainable.

TOOLS FOR UNDERSTANDING EQUITY

Equity Audits to Uncover Equity Gaps

Equity audits are leadership tools that can be developed for any organization and industry to uncover and change systemic barriers that impact the overall success of individuals. Public school systems may develop these institutional assessments to evaluate the quality of instruction or educational programs. Higher education may audit policies, practices and procedures that impact student access, persistence and completion. Business and industry can also use this concept to evaluate hiring and recruitment practices in order to attract diverse candidates, while creating an inclusive culture.

Develop an Equity-Mindset

Researchers associated with the Center for Urban Education at the University of Southern California believe that educational leaders need to become equity-minded and to do this they must start with evaluating the inequitable practices of historical, social, cultural and economic context. The deep-dive or self-reflection for equity-minded leaders can be difficult and uncomfortable but necessary. Future of the community college system and business and industry requires transformational leaders who examine how an equity-mindset can contribute to systemic barriers for students and employees.

Estela Mara Bensimon et al. describe equity-mindedness as a way of thinking and understanding of how policies, practices and procedures within a system can negatively impact the experience of students of color even if they appear to be race neutral. Creating equity in systems that currently repeat historical inequities requires that students and employees be treated differently (Bragg and McCambly 2017).

This will force leaders to reevaluate how resources are accessed and disseminated. Just as community colleges have developed curriculum to train the workforce, we also need to develop professional development opportunities to create a culture of equity. Implicit bias, courageous conversation, and racial equity workshops can foster opportunities for self-reflection and help organizations to create a common language and shared vision for equity.

Close Gaps by Assessing the Organizational Circles

Closing equity gaps is not an easy topic to address, nor put into practice right away. Anyone setting out to do this type of work needs to be patient, gritty, and compassionate. Patience is needed to understand that implementing the equity concept is like any other type of change: a slow process. An unknown author wrote a parable about an admiral of an aircraft carrier who was asked by a reporter how long it would take for the ship to complete a 180 degree turn. The admiral responded, "14 miles." After noticing the look of disappointment on the reporter's face, the admiral added, "I could turn it around in five miles, but the tilt on the deck would cause the aircraft to fall into the ocean." Quick change can be harmful to the desired outcomes of any organization, but change needs to be done expeditiously.

To successfully engage in equity work, a leader must first identify the different circles that make up the organization. Circles include: immediate supporters, investigators, and resisters. Immediate supporters support the cause without hesitation. This group usually makes up about 20 percent of the organization. To keep the momentum going remember to empower this group as much as possible. Investigators require some convincing before they join the cause. Educate the investigators on the benefits of the change to help them keep their minds off the challenges. This group makes up about 60 percent of the organization and need continuous support. Resisters is the remaining circle of an organization and serve as critics. This is where being gritty and compassionate is needed most. Engage but try not to spend a lot of energy on this group. Refrain from letting expended energy that could have been used on immediate stakeholders go to waste.

Leaders must identify the circles within the organization and take action by using the following steps:

- *Self-Assess*. Know the "why" and rehearse different variations of this. Just because one way sounds good to you, does not mean others in the circles will be as accepting.
- *Recruit immediate supporters*. The work is more meaningful and easier when others join the cause.
- *Synergize your "why" with the "why" of your immediate supporters*. This is done to create a powerful message for the investigators to acknowledge and consent to.
- *Ask immediate supporters to help persuade the investigators*.

Plan your work and work your plan, while communicating often to as many stakeholders as possible. Communication is essential in creating a culture of equity.

Workforce Development Professionals as Equity Stakeholders

The history of the community college is embedded with the integration of workforce and economic needs for the community it serves. For decades, community college leaders have worked collaboratively with workforce and economic development boards to effectively plan, develop, and implement programming that prepares students for the local, national, and global workforce. As an active community partner in educational, workforce, and economic development, the community college strives to establish and maintain mutually beneficial relationships.

In 2018, the North Carolina Department of Commerce conducted an employer needs survey to identify gaps between what many of today's workers possess versus the demands of the workplace. More than 2,000 North Carolina businesses participated in the survey. The respondents represented many industries, including healthcare, STEM, and manufacturing. Survey results indicated that North Carolina businesses need a trained labor force with work experience and education relevant to the job. The results also suggested that technical skills, emotional intelligence skills (previously referred to as soft skills), work ethic and reliability are necessary across many business sectors.

The global workforce needs are changing rapidly due to exponential advances in technology (Staat 2019). These rapid changes require more than emotional intelligence or human relations skills for employees of the fourth industrial revolution (Staat 2019). Successful workers need technical competence and emotional intelligence or human relations skills to work in high-demand careers. Successful workforce development professionals and college leaders need to embrace the diversity of the new workforce and consider the barriers to access, persistence and completion these students face, while developing programs to train them.

College and Industry Collaboration

North Carolina, the third largest community college system in the country, is comprised of 58 community colleges. Collaborations in and with complex organizations, even when they share a common purpose or goal, can be difficult. College leadership and industry partners must seek common ground before defining outcomes. Colleges cannot remain set on "ivory tower" objectives and industry must be willing to work with higher education institutions to set reasonable standards. Workforce development must be integrated into the fabric of the college, instead of being viewed as an add-on that has less value than degree programs and transfer rates.

Economic workforce development has been and continues to be a driver of change in community colleges, since the implementation of the Workforce Investment Act, now the Workforce Innovation and Opportunity Act. However, the cost of offering programming in a period of declining federal and state funding has caused many community college leaders to question how to sustain the mission while meeting the needs of business and industry partners. The global workforce needs are changing so rapidly. Advances in technology require more advanced technical and human relations skills.

The ability to harmonize processes and functions across large organizations require a clear mission and vision, as well as a long-term plan for educational training, collaboration with all constituencies and the support and the integration of parallel and complementary structures. Human capital should be the most valuable output of any organization, and leaders must ensure that they value and reward their employees. Recognizing and valuing the contributions of employees not only sustains the company, but also impacts the economy. The coordination of training and development across large, complex organizations, while leveraging institutional capacity, requires coherent processes which acknowledge differences and simultaneously creates commonalities that lead to a sense of shared purpose.

Collaboration to Develop Pathways for Success

In December 2018, the 115th Congress reauthorized the Carl D. Perkins Act. The legislation increases the role of business in funded programs, better aligns Perkins with WIOA, and more fully integrates career pathways programs into the Act. The Guided Pathways/Meta-Majors model partners well with this reauthorization, providing colleges and businesses the opportunity to develop more meaningful opportunities of choice. As organizations become more dynamic, complex, and competitive, leaders will face increasingly conflicting demands.

Higher education teaches leadership behaviors that allow for differences while still meeting the demands of competing interests and needs, both simultaneously and over time. This requires continued college leadership and industry collaboration to develop pathways between curriculum, continuing education, and workforce development programs. Workforce professionals must be flexible in meeting business and industry needs while remaining consistent and dedicated to helping diverse student populations succeed.

CONCLUSION

Meeting the needs of business and industry partners by educating middle-skilled workers for the jobs of the future requires stakeholders to develop an equity-mindset to remain responsive to ever-changing workforce needs. Developing an equity-mindset will require stakeholders to: continuously audit systems, close gaps by assessing and re-assessing organizational circles, encourage workforce development professionals to become equity stakeholders, and collaborate to develop pathways for student success. It also requires organizational change that will undoubtedly be uncomfortable, but necessary. Some will hold on to traditional habits, while others will welcome the challenge. Recognizing the end goal is to develop equitable processes, leaders must work together to develop inclusive environments that stimulate the growth, development and success of all students and future workers.

A SPECIAL ACKNOWLEDGMENT

This chapter has benefited greatly from the recommendations of Dr. Debra Bragg, an expert in the field of community college research. Dr. Bragg was the founding director of the Office of Community College Research and Leadership (OCCRL) at the University of Illinois at Urbana-Champaign where she served for 25 years. Dr. Bragg currently serves as the director of the Community College Research Initiatives group at the University of Washington, in the Center for Experiential Learning and Diversity.

REFERENCES

Bensimon, Estela Mara, Robert Rueda, Alicia C. Dowd, and Frank Harris III. "Accountability, Equity, and Practitioner Learning and Change." *Metropolitan Universities*, 18. No. 3 (2007): 28–45.

Bragg, Debra and Heather McCambly. 2017. "Using Adaptive Equity-Minded Leadership to Bring About Large-scale Change." Washington State Board of Community College and Technical Colleges, Bragg & Associates, Inc., April 20. https://www.sbctc.edu/resources/documents/colleges-staff/programs-services/student-success-center/critical-friend/brief-1-equity-minded-leadership-2017-04-20.pdf

Center for Urban Education, University of Southern California. 2019. "Equity Mindedness." Accessed July 21. https://cue.usc.edu/about/equity/equity-mindedness/

North Carolina Department of Commerce. 2018. "2018 Employer Needs Survey." Accessed August 12. https://files.nc.gov/nccommerce/documents/files/2018-employer-needs-survey.pdf

Staat, Darrel W. 2019. Exponential Technologies: Higher Education in an Era of Serial Disruptions. Lanham: Rowman & Littlefield.

The Vernā Myers Company. 2019. "About Vernā Myers." Accessed August 12. https://learning.vernamyers.com/pages/about-vern-myers

Chapter Eight

Technological Change

Human Adaptation Through Effective Learning

Stephen R. Catt

RAPID RATE OF CHANGE IN TECHNOLOGY AND ITS EFFECTS ON LEARNING

There are compelling reasons for future and incumbent workers to learn continuously. In fact, it is critical that our workers to have training resources available. Community colleges have an opportunity to play increasing roles in this arena but will be competing with a variety of emerging training providers. Understanding and embracing new technologies in learning and manufacturing will combine to successfully lifting the middle class of our nation. If not, other training providers will . . . or worse, our workers will be left behind in this global competition.

Technology is changing at exponential rates, affecting everything we experience. As individuals, organizations, and our country, we can choose to embrace these changes or fight against them. If we choose to embrace them, then we must adapt; to adapt, we must learn and that requires a change in behavior. Community colleges cannot be known as teaching institutions; they must be catalysts for learning. Technology will continue to improve, how people adapt will determine our success. Helping people adapt is community colleges' greatest role.

Community colleges approach training for manufacturers, specifically small and medium-sized manufacturers (SMMs), for two compelling reasons. First, manufacturing is a primary economic generator, which means that in every community, it provides wages, investments, and taxes that support secondary and tertiary activities such as retail, entertainment, education, healthcare, and community infrastructure. Second, our nation's defense, economy, and large corporations depend on them. They are the critical supply chain that provides every part that makes up our planes, vehicles, etc. Large corporations have resources for training, research, and support; SMMs simply do not. Community colleges have the potential to bridge that gap, but few have a sense of urgency or the incentives to accomplish this task. That is why Manufacturing USA Institutes such as ARM seek your help and will support your efforts in serving the training needs of your regional manufacturers.

Organizational change experts will agree that when technological or structural changes occur, computers, tables, chairs, and buildings don't care about the change and will abide with whatever is implemented. Only humans care . . . and are the only 'things' that need to adapt. People, however, have feelings, attachments, history, and a plethora of other challenges that need to be addressed before any change can be successful. Inertia is an important concept in human behavior; a body at rest requires additional energy to begin movement. Once an object (person) is moving, it takes much less energy to keep it moving. The good news is that humans are made to adapt! Our species wins consistently because we observe, learn, adapt, and thrive. Our new technological world today presents similar challenges, but at a pace humans have never confronted before.

ADDRESSING STRATEGIC WORKFORCE CHALLENGES TO ADVANCED MANUFACTURING

The Advanced Robotics for Manufacturing (ARM), www.arminstitute.org, is one of 14 Manufacturing USA Institutes created by the United States government to regain our country's top position in Manufacturing. After extensive research, road mapping sessions with industry and education, and numerous site visits, six strategic workforce challenges determine efforts and investment.

1. Inadequate education system to prepare youth for advanced manufacturing
2. Negative perceptions of robotics and manufacturing
3. Small and medium-sized manufacturers (SMMs) have limited resources to train and upgrade workers
4. The American worker is not prepared or encouraged to continuously learn
5. There is little coordination of effective training initiatives in advanced manufacturing
6. There are regional skill gaps in manufacturing skills

These challenges also affect the missions of our community colleges because they are either attempting to currently address these issues or will be asked to do so very soon. Manufacturing, indeed, our country, is facing major transformations through a variety of simultaneous advancements that demand an educated population that can adapt to new situations quickly. Not only does functional foundational knowledge play an integral role (accredited programs), but constant upgrading of skills to keep up with new technologies (workforce training) will be critical to all our success. Adaptive skills are the new survival skills in this emerging society. Bottom line: We all need to 'learn to learn,' which is not new, but is much more urgent today.

It is disappointing to see the United States education system producing students that fall to 38 out of 71 countries in Math, 24 in Science and Reading. (Pew Research, February 2017). Although there are wonderful "best practices" that are led by teachers throughout our country, the investment in Pre-K–12 public education system is overall abysmal. Unfortunately, the community college system is called to compensate for this lack of foresight by testing every student and placing up to 60 percent of all incoming freshman in college preparatory Math, Writing, and Reading courses. Often overlooked are programs providing skills training to incumbent workers. Companies often contract their local community colleges to develop training programs to teach foundational competencies in math, communication, and professionalism to their workers.

"Why are you sitting there so calmly in your seats?" Henry Kissinger once said to an audience after he had briefed them on a particularly unsettling world situation. "Why aren't you out running in the streets, spreading the alarm?" (Grayson, 25). The situation is extremely serious, if for no other reason our military readiness is placed in jeopardy if all critical equipment and technology are manufactured in other countries.

FUTURISTS PREDICTED RAPID TECHNOLOGICAL CHANGE

Three influential philosophers from the late twentieth century, Alvin Toffler, Malcomb Knowles, and John Naisbitt, provide research and advice for how we should approach learning in the twenty-first century.

Alvin Toffler, the author of *Future Shock*, warned us in the 1970s that our society was about to experience change at a level unprecedented in human history. That there will be some that embrace and keep up with it, and others will be lost to a state of mind he coined "future shock."

> Future shock is a time phenomenon, a product of the greatly accelerated change in society. It arises from the superimposition of a new culture on an old one. It is culture shock in one's own society. But its impact is much worse. For most Peace Corps members, in fact most travelers, have the comforting knowl-

edge that the culture they left behind will be there to return to. The victim of future shock does not. Now imagine not merely an individual but an entire society, an entire generation—including its weakest, least intelligent, and most irrational members—suddenly transported into this new world. The result is mass disorientation, future shock on a grand scale. (Toffler 1970)

Unless we take intentional action, a great majority will rebel against these changes. We are currently seeing this phenomenon through groups voting against change, clinging to an idealistic notion of simpler lives, as if we could only reverse these trends and go back in time. Without an engaged, educated population, progress will at minimum be slowed, if not inhibited. Workers who are willing to learn and adapt to new technologies will be harder to find unless we can change public perception to an acceptance of technological progress. Creating a bridge across this Future Shock chasm can be a service provided to our society by community colleges.

Picture our civilization evolving over time in juxtaposition to how long we live. People's lifespans are now greater than eighty years, while at the same time societies experience transformations at an unprecedented pace. Humans, as a species, have never had to adapt so rapidly to pervasive and overwhelming change as in our current era. Most change has exponential technological innovations at its core. The only antidote is continuous learning.

Malcomb Knowles is known as the father of Andragogy, how adults learn. Instead of assuming a person has a 'tabula rasa' or blank slate for a brain, adult learners have experiences and prior learning that need to connect before accepting any new behavior. Without acknowledging a person's prior experiences coming into a new situation, most new information will be deemed inconsequential and ignored. Knowles identified seven principles of adult learning: (1) Adults must want to learn, (2) they learn only when they need to do so, (3) they learn by doing, (4) they need to focus on problem solving, (5) prior experience influences how and what they learn, (6) adults learn best in informal settings, and (7) they want guidance as equal partners in the learning process. Until we transform from pedagogical (how children learn) curriculum and methods into andragogy, many adult learners will be bored and disconnected from learning opportunities. It is time to create an education system that places these concepts as the foundation of learning, not theories that treat workers like children.

John Naisbitt, who wrote *Megatrends* in 1980, had a number of chapters devoted to the trends that would influence the future. Most have proven correct, but one chapter influences how we should train in this new age more than any other . . . high tech, high touch. Humans demand engagement with other humans. As our technology continues to evolve and transform everything in its path, humans still need to connect with each other. When we delve into on-line education, apps that provide information and training, and other types of technology driven training; we must involve human interaction. Hands-on training and experiences enhance learning on equipment and in unique environments . . . but implied in this aspect are the interactions with experienced workers that provide role models and individual advice. Only then does the new learned behavior have accountability, credibility, and sustainability.

There is a Buddhist quote, "The teacher will appear when the student is ready." That is a wonderful sentiment, but rarely does it happen without strategic action. In today's expectation of instant gratification, we need to be increasingly adept to create training that students can access when they need it. We need to be intentional about creating repositories of knowledge that can be accessed upon request, in ways that fulfill that unique individual with the need they have in that moment. When a worker needs to learn something to solve a problem, they want an immediate solution. Many find a YouTube video of someone showing them how to solve it. That is a great example of the beginning . . . but what about the theories and foundational knowledge it takes to understand that technology so that the worker can effectively troubleshoot, invent, and apply that technology to other aspects of production? That is our challenge as educators.

SPECIFIC COMMUNITY COLLEGE CHALLENGES

ARM has identified six major challenges in Education and Workforce Development that was described at the beginning of this chapter. Every one of them is important, but two have more relevance for community colleges; #3- Small and medium-sized manufacturers do not have the resources to train workers and #4- American Workers are not prepared for continuous training. These are your calls to action!

SMMs are in a day to day fight for survival to sell and fulfill orders. Although they are a critical component to the supply chain for the largest corporations such as Boeing, GM, etc., they do not have resources to upskill their employees to keep up with new technologies and processes. Therefore, an infrastructure of learning must be implemented that (a) creates a trusted awareness of training resources to both SMMs and workers, (b) determines competency and skill needs at all levels of the manufacturing process, (c) develops unique curricula that meets a continuum of immediate to long term needs through a stackable learning system, (d) is accessible to the current and potential worker that considers cost, duration, scheduling, location, and sometimes even basic life needs such as food and child care, and (e) is constantly updated through employer and worker feedback as well as research about new technologies. The ladder of opportunity must reach to ground level in order to capture the full potential of a region's workforce.

Much of this effort falls on a responsive community college, but every region has complementary agencies that play roles in developing an effective infrastructure of learning. Also note that every region is unique! Career Services, Workforce Investment Boards, Manufacturing Extension Programs, Chambers of Commerce, Foundations, State and Federal agencies, Proprietary Technical Training Institutes, Vo-Techs, and other resources are available. However, if there is not an effective infrastructure and no other organization is coordinating these efforts, then it is incumbent upon the community college to take an active leadership role in its creation. Every region is unique and is at various levels of maturity. Also, what works in other regions of the country may not work in your region; there is no cookie-cutter solution or playbook that will guarantee success.

What does a successful infrastructure of learning look like? The outcomes would include a large percentage of the working population involved in some type of education, training, or upskilling that benefits both the individual and employer. People have access through awareness of credible and appropriate programs, reasonable expense, proximity to home or work, reasonable duration of the class, and flexible times. SMMs participate in the creation of training programs that meet their needs which reduce turnover, enrich their employees, allow them to adapt to new technologies faster, and create a support system among like-minded owners. The region will be more attractive to new companies and workers because flexibility and adaptability become selling points for economic development

Make no mistake, ARM wants every region to be successful and will assist through every means at our disposal.

Failure is, unfortunately, an option in far too many well-intentioned training programs. We all are aware of successful programs, but there are few that sustain themselves for very long. So, how, and why, do successful programs fail? First, upon creation of new programs there was little thought into sustainability. Some begin by obtaining a large grant that provides an infusion of startup funding for the program. If the funding lasts, the program is successful, but fades soon after the funding stream evaporates. Second, leadership either has turnover or loses interest. Strategic priorities within an institution determine where funding, marketing, and support are invested. Leadership turnover can be deadly to a program if it is unknown, misunderstood, has little ROI for the institution, or is outside of a leader's comfort zone of expertise. Third, a passionate advocate departs from the program. Usually there is at least one person or a small department that supports a program by providing guidance, history, coordination, and publicity. Without a succession strategy, once this person(s) leave(s), the program dissipates because it gets lost in a larger system of competing priorities.

CONCLUSION

In conclusion, community colleges should:

- Attract talent: Get involved with your community and region through agencies that are involved in training, educating, attracting, and developing the workforce. Where there is a gap, provide leadership. Build strong relationships that promote new manufacturing jobs because community colleges cannot do this on their own, and it is not their only priority. However, community colleges can provide a neutral, credible voice that can provide local expertise. Hosting seminars, convening solution summits, and bringing in expert speakers are additional tools that have proven their effectiveness.
- Train new workers: Work closely with both local manufacturers and credible national associations to create curriculum that is industry recognized and continuously updated. Credit programs must obtain input from non-credit workforce departments, usually through contracted training so that curriculum and training equipment can be updated based on real-world manufacturing needs. Certifications and Associate Degrees need to have constant updates based on input from industry advisory teams, regional surveys, industry associations, and your own workforce training department. Ideally, every semester should have several improvements based on this industry input. Technology and Manufacturing programs will graduate unprepared workers if not constantly updated. Finally, marketing and admissions need to have specific strategies to recruit students into these programs. Most Tech and Manufacturing programs have 100 percent placement of successful graduates into their fields of study, and yet community colleges typically do not capitalize on these amazing opportunities.
- Train incumbent workers: Manufacturing workers in the United States have not been accustomed to an environment of continuous training. Large corporations have resources and internal expertise to train their direct employees. Some have their own 'universities' because they acknowledge how important educated workers are to their success. Small manufacturers do not have those resources and depend on external training resources, namely community colleges. Workforce development departments at all community colleges are critical to providing training for most of the US supply chain.
- Create and maintain relevant programs: There are thousands of curriculum, certifications, credentials, and degrees. It is imperative that community colleges do their homework in determining what credentials they will use to prove their graduates and worker training have relevance to employers. Does industry not only endorse, but use a credential to hire and

promote their workers? Is the credential updated to keep up with new technologies and latest procedures? Is safety an underlying and constant theme throughout the lessons? Do students and workers have easy access to a user-friendly platform? Finally, is there a rigorous process that allows a credible advisory board consisting of subject matter experts, industry leaders, and educators to evaluate and recommend improvements, additions, and omissions necessary to continuously adapt to a changing manufacturing environment?

REFERENCES

Grayson, C. J. and O'Dell, C; *American Business: A Two-Minute Warning*. New York: Macmillan Publishers, 1988.

Knowles, M. *The Modern Practice of Adult Education: From Pedagogy to Andragogy.*, Englewood Cliffs, NJ: Cambridge Adult Education Prentice Hall Regents, 1988.

Naisbitt, J., *Megatrends: Ten New Directions Transforming Our Lives*: New York: Warner Books, 1982.

Toffler, A. *Future Shock*. New York: Bantam Books, 1970.

Chapter Nine

Embedded Industry Credentials

A Measure of Student Success

Bryan Albrecht and Matt Janisin

TACTICAL APPROACH TO EMBEDDING CERTIFICATIONS

The nation's economy is at a crossroads where the need for workers is at its greatest peak and the population demographics are not able to fill the demand. This dilemma is causing disruption in the way education and workforce providers are preparing students for jobs and careers. John R. McKernan Jr., President of the U.S. Chamber of Commerce Foundation stated, "Today, the stability of the American economy is facing a serious threat. The skills gap is impacting the ability of our companies to compete and grow in today's economy while shortcomings in our education and workforce development systems continue to widen the gap."

In a recent survey by Adecco it was reported that 92 percent of executives believe there is a serious gap in workforce skills and nearly half are missing out on growth opportunities as a result. The Milwaukee based Manpower Group confirmed this survey and reported that 40 percent of U.S. employers are struggling to fill jobs. This crossroad is in many ways a crisis on the American Dream and the fulfillment of the desire for meaningful work. Left unchanged, the supply of skilled workers will continue to decline, leaving over 6 million jobs vacant by the year 2025. The skills gap is real and is one of our nation's greatest threats to American Competitiveness, both today and in the future.

This chapter will highlight how industry partnerships and embedded industry credentials are serving as a bridge between the skilled worker shortage and workforce productivity. We begin with a perspective that employers can control the greatest currency in today's education and workforce programming: jobs. Jobs must be at the beginning, middle and end of any education or training program. Without a productive job the relevance of the experience is diminished. Employers can drive investments, outcomes and skills taught in our schools, colleges and universities. This supply chain influence benefits individuals, institutions and businesses.

To fully appreciate the employers' role, we must first look at new principles and strategies for talent development management. In a white paper recently published by the U.S Chamber of Commerce Foundation, three foundation principles serve as the base for a new, employer-led education and workforce strategy:

- Employers drive value creation: Employers play a new leadership role as the end- customer in closing the skills gap for those jobs most critical to their competitiveness.
- Employers organize and manage scalable network partnerships: Employers organize and manage flexible and responsive talent pipelines in partnership with their preferred education and workforce providers.
- Employers measures and incentives drive performance: Employers work collaboratively with their partners to develop measures and incentives designed to reinforce and improve performance across all partners.

These principles applied require all the stakeholders—employers, providers, students, workers and policymakers—involved in managing a talent pipeline to rethink their role and how they engage with one another in the talent supply chain. Once employers begin to understand their role as the end - customers in managing talent supply chain partnerships, they can reshape the education and workforce systems as an extended chain of talent providers that prepare learners for careers in the most responsive and effective way possible.

CASE STUDY: NATIONAL COALITION OF CERTIFICATION CENTERS (NC3)

The National Coalition of Certification Centers (NC3) demonstrates the potential industry and education partnerships must unlock the growth in industry recognized skill credentials and up-skilling the American workforce.

"Our greatest potential strength in the global competition for jobs remains the American workforce. The best way to enable that workforce in this competition is technical education. I am convinced the work of NC3 has never been more important. It is imperative to secure our nation's viability in the global economy," Nick Pinchuck, Chairman and Chief Executive Officer, Snap on, Incorporated.

Founded in 1920 and headquartered in Kenosha, Wisconsin, Snap on is a leading global innovator, manufacturer and marketer of tools, equipment, diagnostics, repair information and systems solutions for professional users performing critical tasks. Snap on has a storied history in partnering with education. Gateway Technical College, also located in Kenosha, Wisconsin, was founded in 1911 and has been a partner with Snap on since early 1960s.

The Gateway Technical College—Snap on partnership evolved into a comprehensive and strategic relationship with a shared belief in the importance of career and technical education and the importance of portable, stackable industry credentials. Snap on, a company whose growth is driven by innovation that depends on the underlying technical capability, values the importance of education at all levels in creating the intellectual capital that American companies need to compete. This belief pointed the way to a model with national prominence while at the same time preserving a local impact. As a result, the National Coalition of Certification Centers was formed, and Gateway began training and certifying high school teachers and community and technical college instructors in Snap on diagnostics skills.

It is imperative that education and business work together to advance a common agenda to drive local economies and sustain a highly skilled and productive workforce. Amplifying this effort are the organizations that influence policy and workforce investment. Organizations like workforce and economic development boards, local school boards, chambers of commerce and training providers. Business and industry leaders have a perspective that can drive curriculum and training standards. The delivery of these standards can further be influenced by local advisory committees, instructor training and credential validation by recognized industry organizations.

Current job-skill requirements and assessing future skill development opportunities is a shared responsibility between industry and education. Industry credentials that have meaning and measure the skill attainment of students or incumbent workers is essential to assuring relevancy in today's technical education programming. Portable, stackable and embedded credentials have been discussed for a decade without agreement on how best to accomplish the end goal for workers.

The most common description of stackable credentials outlined in *Inside Higher Ed* (May 2016) by Jimmie Williamson and Matthew Pittinsky states; "over a lifetime of learning, individuals can assessable. Or stack, a series of traditional degree-based and/or nontraditional credentials-certificates, certifications, licenses, badges, apprenticeships and more that recognize achievements and provide an accurate assessment of knowledge, skills and abilities."

The challenge of developing a model that accomplishes all aspects of the workforce credentialing was the driving force behind the NC3 embedded model for student success.

Tactical Approach to Embedding Certifications

In today's high tech and ever-changing world employers are seeking candidates based on not just what they know, but also what they can do when joining an organization. Gateway seeks to provide opportunities for our graduates to differentiate themselves by earning industry recognized certifications along with their academic credentials, so they can showcase both what they know and what they can do. The goal is to provide this opportunity for *all* students, which can be difficult with other certification platforms.

First, the NC3 certifications are designed in a modular fashion that allows them to be easily integrated into existing curriculum and enhance the learning experience. This makes is easier for instructors to fit the certifications into already time constrained programs. The certification content is not always "new" but instead provides a better and more standardized way of teaching some common content with the added benefit of a third-party industry partner verifying the curriculum and skill set.

Second, NC3 certifications do not cost "per test" like many certification models. The school's investment is upfront in both equipment and instructor training, but after these investments are made, there are no ongoing costs to issue certifications to the students. With the individual certification exams being free, 100 percent of the students can participate and instructors can truly embed these into their existing curriculum. The certification exams are not "extra" or "optional," but instead a regular exam that serves as both graded assignment for the class and a resume builder for the student. No student gets left behind with the certification opportunity open to all (see figure 9.1).

RESULTS

The first full year of integrating the Snap-on diagnostic certifications was 2008 with about five schools participating. In 2008 Gateway issued just over 50 certifications and the NC3 grand total was about 70 issued certifications. Since 2008 NC3 has added many more industry partners, equating too many more certifications, and the number of schools has grown tremendously.

As of April 2019, the total number of student NC3 certifications issued now stands at over 202,000 from over 600 schools and colleges. During this same time Gateway has issued almost 9,000 certifications total and has averaged over 1,700 certifications per year since 2016. Scalability and accessibility are a couple key results NC3 has delivered on. The 120,000 students in the NC3 certification site, who have earned over 202,000 certifications, show this model has the ability to quickly grow and adapt to rapidly changing industry needs while remaining accessible to resource strained schools and colleges.

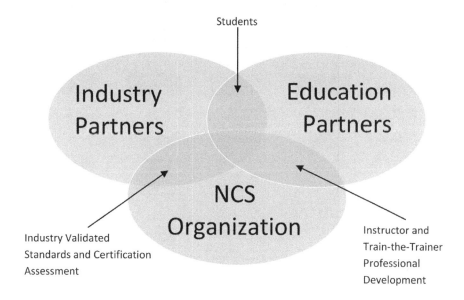

Figure 9.1. NC3 Industry Collaboration Model. *Bryan Albrecht and Matt Janisin.*

The following chart is an example of Gateway Technical College Career Pathway for Automotive Technology. The chart demonstrates how NC3 Industry Certifications add value to the academic credentials along the career consortium. Career pathways provide a "road map" for students through post-secondary education and training programs organized as a series of steps leading to successively higher credentials and employment opportunities. Each step is designed to prepare individuals for the next level of employment with market value credentials (see figures 9.2 and 9.3).

CONCLUSION

Rightly so, student needs and outcomes are the main focus of many educational initiatives, but unfortunately the classroom and the instructor are often overlooked. The instructor is the most influential variable in a student's experience and overall success. Student engagement and technical skill attainment is driven by the instructor and the facilities in which they both interact. The partnership with Snap-on and NC3 has helped Gateway, and many other colleges, transform our facilities into high tech areas of inspiration and provided our instructors with the professional development they needed to be comfortable and confident in the classroom while teaching emerging technology. This has led to Gateway students earning several industry-recognized certifications to augment their academic credentials. Hav-

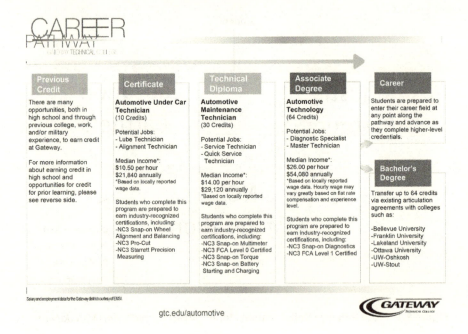

Figure 9.2. Career Pathway: Automotive Technology. *Bryan Albrecht and Matt Janisin.*

ing both on their resume differentiates them from a typical college graduate with only academic credentials. If you want to have a positive impact on students, start with supporting the instructor and the classroom environment. NC3 and their industry partners do this better than anyone.

The mission of NC3 is to serve as a value-driven organization and the future model for Career and Technical Education, creating highly skilled, job ready professionals through a growing network of educational partners and global industry leaders. This evolving organization has been recognized by the U.S. Department of Labor, The National Association of Workforce Boards, American Association of Community Colleges, Association for Career and Technical Education, Society of Manufacturing Engineers and the Manufacturing Skill Standards Council as a key partner in building America's workforce. To learn more about how your school can become involved in offering industry credentials search the NC3.net website.

ABOUT GATEWAY TECHNICAL COLLEGE

Gateway Technical College was founded in 1911 with the mission to provide quality technical education to the residents of Southeast Wisconsin. Gateway

Embedded Industry Credentials 79

Figure 9.3. Career Pathway: Automotive Technology. *Bryan Albrecht and Matt Janisin.*

is one of sixteen technical college districts in the state and serves over 20,000 students annually. With 60 degree and diploma programs and 200 industry certification credentials Gateway is a critical component to the regional workforce.

REFERENCES

Carnevale, A.P., Rose, S.J., Hanson, A.R. (22012), Certficates: Gateway to gainful employement and college degree. Georgetown Center on Education and the Workforce, Washington D.C. Retrieved from http://knowledgecenter.completionbydesign.org/sites/default/files/%20Carnevale%20Rose%202012.pdf

"Competency-based Education." Educause, Accessed May 20, 2019, www.library.educause.edu

"Managing the Talent Pipleline: A New Approach to Closing the Skills Gap," U.S. Chamber of Commerce Foundation, 2014, p. 13. Accessed May 10, 2019. http://www.uschamberfoundation

McMernan, John, R, Talent Pipeline Management: An Employer-led Solution to Closing the Skills Gap. Advancing a Jobs Driven Economy, 2015, STEM connector, p. 6.

"National Coalition of Certification Centers website." Accessed May 12, 2019. www.NC3.net

"The Skills Gap and the State of the Economy." Recruiting Career Blog. October 29, 2013. Accessed May 14, 2019. http://blog.adeccousa.com/the-skills-gap-and-the-state-of-the-economy/

"The Talent Shortage Continues: How the Ever Changing Role of HR Can Bridge the Gap," Manpower Group, 2014, p. 4, http://www.manpowergroup.us/campaigns/talent-shortage-2014/assets/pdf/2014_Talent_Shortage_WP_US.pdf

Chapter Ten

Learning While Working

Paul Schreffler

This chapter is focused on the many forms of Work-Based Learning (WBL) in community college settings. So that you can best use the information presented in this chapter, we have organized it by providing a bulleted list of tips, placed at the beginning, for building and sustaining WBL programs. In addition, we provide a "top ten" set of best practices, placed at the end of the chapter, to help you implement work-based learning in your organization.

These tips provide valuable insight, and examples of successful models to explore, as you seek to incorporate work-based learning into your college programs. The main text of the chapter contains ten sub-headings in the "how-to" section, using the same number and heading name used in the list of best practices. In that way, you can quickly locate more detailed information about the research, rationale and process for that particular point, provided within the preceding text.

TIPS FOR BUILDING WORK-BASED LEARNING (WBL) PROGRAMS

- Learn the process and related details of Federal/State Registered Apprenticeship programs. This long-established system provides a model with proven success. It offers thousands of already-defined job classifications and detailed information about the skills and competencies required in those occupations.
- Understand the pros and cons of this federal system. Be aware of and open to the unique perspective of your corporate customer when including any such program in a workforce development solution.

- Work with your state apprenticeship agency to access help to implement a program. Some states have reengineered such services, so assistance may be coordinated regionally or even through your statewide community college system.
- A single company, a consortium of companies or a college can be an official apprenticeship sponsor. This can ease the administrative burden for a company to implement a program.
- Some regions also have public or private nonprofit entities that can serve as a sponsor. Be sure that you know the players and their respective capacities in your region, so that you can steer a potential project in the right direction, to maximize benefits for the company and apprentice.
- Recognize that the company is the driver of any apprenticeship/WBL decision.
- Both "RA" (Registered Apprenticeship) and "AltA" (industry-defined alternative apprenticeship/WBL) can work, depending on the unique circumstances within a company and your local environment.
- Recognize that knowledge management is a common challenge for companies today. The mentor-mentee relationship in WBL is a proven method for effectively transferring critical knowledge assets, both explicit and tacit, to the incoming workforce.
- Consider the cost and benefit for all parties in the relationship. Upfront, make sure that the company is clear about the investment (of both time and money), and its potential return, in implementing a comprehensive WBL program. The following steps are critical in this ROI analysis:[1]

    1. Determine the total costs, both fixed and variable, of the proposed WBL program.
    2. Determine the costs of the counterfactual scenario—any alternative hiring/training methods used if the program had not been available.
    3. Compare the above two scenarios.
    4. Look across the company for data that can be used to measure program benefits.
    5. Keep in mind other changes happening at the company and its environment that affect performance.
    6. Analyze and share the data across the company to improve buy-in.
    7. Continue to analyze cost/benefit and results data to drive program improvement.
    8. Consider industry-sector models for program structure.
    9. Become aware of successful multi-company models that have shown success. Reach out to these organizations for assistance.

- These models can also alleviate some of the administrative burden for single companies.

- Recognize that sector-based models will require corporate engagement in the leadership and management of the program.
- Leverage the federal focus on growing apprenticeships by accessing resources available through state-level projects.
- Become informed about, engage and integrate with state or regional initiatives designed to facilitate apprenticeship program support and development.
- Commit time and effort to contribute your leadership to such initiatives. You don't have to drive the bus, but make sure that the perspective of your institution is included as a strategy is developed.
- Ensure that your college's leadership is informed of strategic planning for the advancement of apprenticeships, so that its positive benefits can be considered, prioritized, coordinated and implemented within your own institution's strategy.
- Work with state-level partners to assess data system capacity and labor market criteria/metrics. Seek consensus on whose data will be the basis for analysis and decision-making.
- To affect meaningful change, support from top-level leadership of all partners is critical. Be informed and prepared to show data on the results of WBL. Research data on both student success and institutional growth is available and continues to grow. Subscribe to publications focused on this field to remain informed on the results of current studies.
- Include faculty in any and all planning.
- Faculty are key to the success of any educational program, and this is especially true for apprenticeships and WBL programs.
- You already have faculty engaged in programmatic review for reasons of accreditation or the development of customized content, *but* -
- WBL demands a deeper level of employer input for the definition and delivery of related technical instruction.
- WBL also demands an increased level of awareness and communication between faculty and those providing supervision of students in the workplace.
- Include student services in the planning and implementation of apprenticeship/WBL programs.
- Research shows that these, like other college programs, are dependent upon the provision of high-quality, coordinated student services.
- Support through coaching, mentoring and tutoring have dramatic impact on student persistence in these programs.
- Financial support provided by paid internships and other student benefits (paid tuition and books, or other incentives) must be coordinated between student, company and college. This may require innovative thinking while examining existing financial aid/payment systems.
- Work and learn programs require different class scheduling.

- Students' work schedule is a critical element of WBL programs. Classroom and laboratory times must be planned to allow for effective learning in school and coordinated with the timely application of that learning at work.
- Shift work, multi-company programs and other factors can complicate scheduling. Many programs are built around a full-time model, where students are either at school or at work on a 40-hour work week.
- Scheduling may require modification within existing student/course management systems.
- Faculty course load and time/effort considerations can also be contractual factors.
- WBL programs offer an opening to improve learning assessment.
- Assessment of any work/learn program must include input from the employer to gauge learning within the workplace.
- This requires upfront collaborative planning of the content and timing of learning assessments, and the method and frequency of communication between company and faculty.
- Timely communication between college and company can identify and rectify student performance problems. Planning and agreement on policy for workplace contingencies is critical for student management.
- Measures of student success include not only degree completion but may also include a job and potential income growth. Does your college's institutional effectiveness data include such criterion in its dataset?
- Include your corporate partner in an integrated recruitment strategy.
- Companies have a big incentive to work with your college to attract the right candidates.
- The company may know the specific target market better than your recruiters, and can help greatly with outreach, messaging and candidate selection.
- Note that student selection methodology may also require modification of current college policy, program entrance requirements and related back-end systems.
- Some WBL programs allow students to graduate with a degree without the attendant debt, immediately gain full-time employment with a family-sustaining wage and have a fast track to promotion within a company. Once you have a track record, be sure to leverage this message within your college's marketing strategy.
- Ensure that the curricular content, terms, conditions and outcomes of any WBL are outlined in written agreements.
- Such agreements should clearly spell out expectations and responsibilities of both the company and the college.

- Student responsibilities and terms of employment (including hours of work, performance expectations, wages, tuition reimbursement requirements, etc.) should also be executed between the company and the student.
- Keep an eye out for technological advances in learning.
- New educational technology can be used in the classroom and workplace to enhance training and lower its cost. The application of simulation, virtual reality (VR) and artificial intelligence (AI) is changing the landscape of education and can be used to great effect in supplementing WBL.
- This, too, requires innovative thinking and the willingness of faculty and administrators to pilot, learn and adapt.

OVERVIEW

Learning within the workplace is nothing new, yet there is renewed focus on how experiential or work-based learning can be utilized and expanded to solve the lack of skills within the labor force. Examples can be found, across many cultures, of formal and informal processes for transferring the essential working knowledge of specific crafts and trades. Apprenticeships within the guilds of Europe and the master/disciple relationships of Asia are examples that reach far back into history.

The somewhat familial, one-on-one relationship between the tutor and mentor during these examples is noteworthy, and should be instructive as we proceed to define such models in our present age. Without a doubt, people learn in many ways—gaining knowledge and skills within classroom and laboratory settings in the traditional education system, while also applying, reinforcing and expanding their learning in on-the-job environments throughout their careers. However, the community of practice in higher education currently lacks the following critical elements:

- A common definition of work-based learning,
- A forum to share best practices in this arena,
- Strategies to scale up programs that are proven to work, and
- A platform to share data that can help businesses, workers, schools and students choose good models for solving the current employment gap.

In this chapter, we will explore how workforce development professionals can use both age-old and new methods of learning to build upon their efforts to address the critical skills gap evident in today's challenging labor market. The topics presented here will focus on the what, why and how of effective work-based education.

As practitioners, we must ask a crucial first question: if there is a challenge in preparing people for jobs, whose responsibility is it to solve the problem? This may seem obvious, but there is great debate as to where the academic and programmatic responsibilities lie. Is addressing the gap in technical and employability skills the responsibility of the individual, of government, of the education system, or of the business/private sector?

Many feel that the responsibility lies within each one of these players, and that progress can only be made if all stakeholders recognize and contribute to the solution. Apprenticeship and other models of work-based learning have been touted as a solution, with increased support by both governments and industries across the globe. Yet coordination of such efforts has been lacking, and this is where the workforce development practitioner has a potential role to play. The partnerships inherent within this work are quite challenging but have been proven to be effective when collaboration between stakeholders is fostered and facilitated.

WHAT IS WORK-BASED LEARNING?

The scientific method demands that the first step in proposing a theory aimed at solving any problem is to clearly define it—thereby giving structure to the ways in which we investigate and document the results. As we seek to identify the outcomes, positive or negative, to any WBL model that is applied to the problem of the skills gap, we run into our first dilemma—the lack of agreement on terms, and some confusion as to how we define the different "treatments" of this kind of learning.

Listing the ways in which such work/learn experiences are defined, we find a wide range of terms: practicum, apprenticeship, internship, cooperative education, clinical practice, mentorship, externship, assistantship, fellowship, traineeship, residency, job shadowing, entrepreneurial experience, school-based enterprise, service learning, on-the-job training (OJT), fieldwork, and experiential learning.

Certainly, each of these can be broadly defined as an educational strategy that provides students with real-life experience within a workplace environment. Each is structured in some way that integrates both academic and technical knowledge, and thus provides an opportunity to provide direct workplace application and skill development. Each model deliberatively seeks to merge theory with practice in order to improve learning and employability. The best of these models acknowledges the intersection of explicit and tacit forms of learning. Yet the differences between methodologies make it not only difficult to agree on terms, but also to define outcomes and compare results.

The higher education community has used work and learn models for decades, especially in certain industry sectors. The required clinical experience within the nursing education pathway, for one, provides highly defined structure and outcomes that have proven to be effective in preparing students for immediate employment in the field.

The Registered Apprenticeship (RA) model, defined and managed through the US Department of Labor and affiliated state organizations, is a system with a clearly stated structure and process, which includes a methodology to identify the length of the program, appropriate and incremental wage levels, and the related technical instruction (RTI) that accompanies the work experience. The growth in the number of apprenticeships in the US, both registered and non-registered, has been the result of favorable policy and fiscal support by both the current and previous federal administrations. Once perceived as solely a function of trade unions, a broad number of sponsor companies have adopted RA as one solution to the workforce pipeline problem.

This has begun to evolve the apprenticeship model beyond its prior perception. Indeed, there are more than a thousand apprenticeable occupations within the RA system that span well beyond the old image of trade-union jobs in construction, manufacturing or transportation. Formal apprenticeships similar to the United States' RA model exist at a much larger scale in other countries, with Germany, the United Kingdom, Australia and Ireland in the lead. Australia, for example, has a unified system of apprenticeship that provides consistent policy, focused support and training resources. This country is a beneficial resource for any scholar/practitioner in the field, as it has a unified data system that encompasses all students, from primary school though college, with many critical data points on apprenticeship that enhances research and analysis of this model of experiential learning. Given its ability to gather and assess longitudinal data, its regular reports on the outcomes and efficacy of apprenticeship programs across Australia are highly recommended reading if you are interested in scaling such efforts here in the US.

Workforce development professionals and faculty at American colleges are regularly engaged with companies through other models, like internships, which are initiated, defined and structured through our ongoing work in finding solutions to fill the workforce pipeline. These "treatments" are often arrived at through collaboration with existing educational programs. The best have been designed with the related work experience in close alignment to the content of the program, with employers providing input on the content of such a program.

Typically built on a case-by-by case basis with either a single employer or consortium of companies within a specific industry sector, an internship's work and learn experience is variable by program. The terms and outcomes of the engagement are, at best, outlined in written agreements between all parties. This model thereby provides a great deal of flexibility, yet that variability presents challenges in assessing the success of the internship model overall. Scaling such a model is thereby more difficult, as the case-by-case methodology is by its nature time and relationship dependent.

WHY SHOULD WE CONSIDER WBL STRATEGIES?

Current labor market statistics show a clear disconnect between supply and demand. Low official unemployment rates in many areas of the country reflect high demand for labor overall, yet there is a persistent mismatch between the supply of skilled workers and the occupational types and/or skills needed by those companies. Several market factors contribute to this gap, including the increasingly global nature of trade within the marketplace. The rapid development of technology and the skills required to work with these new tools is also a significant contributor to the problem.

Colleges and universities struggle to meet the need, while recognizing that most of the employees hired since the Great Recession have been those with more than a high school education. Yet higher education is still locked in a "supply-side" paradigm, with a focus of attracting and then turning out students with credentials that are sometimes outdated and often not specifically aligned with the needs of the current workplace. The efforts of community colleges to redesign its products in a more "demand-driven" model are still in the formative stage, and the progress of those efforts is highly dependent upon forward-thinking leaders. At this point, successes at aligning programmatic response to the new labor market landscape are more episodic than systemic.

This environment has not gone unnoticed by the general public. The trend of disinvestment by government in public higher education, and the fact that most families access college education through those same publicly funded institutions, has led to rapidly increasing costs in tuition and fees for those families who send students to our colleges. Even though the data continues to show that higher education returns significant lifetime value for the investment, the growing percentage of family income devoted to this investment is now being reexamined. Once seen as the only way to win, people are now deferring or declining, largely though an affordability rationale, the opportunity to gain further education beyond high school. This does not bode well for any of our institutions or for the capacity of our workforce.

Yet work and learn models may provide a counter to this reluctance by both families and the employer to engage in the further education of our workforce. The most successful model, from a potential student's financial standpoint, is the Registered Apprenticeship. It is not only a WBL solution; it is by its nature a work-first solution. This is a critical point, and one that cannot be dismissed either from a personal benefit standpoint or an element of any related marketing pitch. Entry into an apprenticeship comes with a regular paycheck, and the RA model even builds in a reasonable increase in wages that reflect an apprentice's rising productivity through the skills gained over time in the program.

From the student standpoint, other WBL models, like internships, have the potential for wage payment during the workplace experience. There have been multiple policy determinations by the federal Department of Labor in regard to the intern/employer relationship and the related issue of wage payment, predicated on the benefit to the employer while the intern is working. This has reduced the incidence of non-paid internships across the board in recent years, due to the risk undertaken by companies that they could be sued for remuneration for productive work. A liberalization of that policy was recently issued by the federal agency, but insufficient time has elapsed to quantify any resultant corporate HR decisions in regard to paid versus unpaid internships.

From the employer's viewpoint, a critical question remains as to whether any work-and-learn model creates value from a business perspective. Both sides of the calculus for the return on investment—the real benefits and costs of work-based learning—must be quantified in order to defend and sell this as a solution to the workforce pipeline problem. Scholarly analysis of the ROI of workplace learning is scant, and the studies that have been done have mostly concentrated on the benefits to the worker or society as a whole, rather than how this practice affects the business that adopts such a practice.

The research on the ROI issue is difficult for several reasons. One potential problem is that often the data that is needed to quantify and analyze bottom-line benefits - like the productivity of an individual worker - may exist in separate, disconnected internal systems. A good example of this is that the wage and hour data that exists in the HR/payroll department (business costs) may not be aligned with measures of individual production within the workplace (business benefits). The subjective nature of HR performance reviews also makes it difficult to measure the economic output of any one employee, let alone to accurately quantify other potential benefits such as the reduction of turnover or even the positive effect on costs due to reductions in errors or mistakes by a more skilled apprentice. Although firms realize the general problem of accessing and training a qualified workforce, they may not combine their own internal data sets to better examine how their worker hiring and training practices affect productivity measures.

The most prevalent model of work-based learning in higher education exists in the allied health field. The practice of clinical education pervades this sector, and it is seen as a "gold standard" of technical education - with accreditation mandates for this work-learn element in place for most nursing and other allied health programs. Linking knowledge and skill development through mentored practice in a real-world environment, the clinical rotations for students in AH professions have traditionally been used to expose students to hands-on interaction with patients and clinical teams. It facilitates the application of knowledge learned in the classroom, as well as the integration of skills developed in college laboratory or simulation settings.

Beyond bridging higher education and the workplace and gaining clinical experience, students learn problem-solving along with ethical decision-making. But what is known about the business value of this long-used practice? Similar to work and learn practices in other industries, studies of clinical placement sites in AH fields describe a range of costs associated with hosting students. Clinical staff in this industry noted increased time working with students and decreased productivity due to supervisory responsibility.[2] They also report increased costs for materials and supplies.[3]

Research literature also notes additional stress on staff due to their supervisory responsibility, combined with the frustration that comes from working with difficult or unprepared students.[4] Formal cost-benefit and cost-effectiveness analyses to identify the economics of clinical education have met with limited success, due to the issues of accurately identifying cost and benefit drivers.[5] Although it has traditionally been seen, on the basis of anecdotal evidence, as a costly endeavor, the practice of clinical education has not been shown by the research to be a significant cost to health care businesses.[6]

To help answer this question, the Clinical Education Task Force (CETF) of the Association of Schools of Allied Health Professions (ASAHP) performed a qualitative study with the aim of gathering the opinions of healthcare employers to better understand the importance, benefits, obstacles, and evolving issues related to allied health (AH) clinical education from the employers' perspective.[7]

The employers reported a major recruitment benefit by retaining the students as employees, with the clinical experience giving the company a long-term look at the student, ensuring a better fit as well as decreased on-boarding time and costs. In addition, the study found a non-monetary benefit—students often brought a fresh perspective to the clinical site. This new energy, new information, and knowledge of current best practice models in the profession tended to keep current staff "on their toes." Interaction with the students also provided leadership opportunities for current employees to hone their skills as potential supervisors.

On the other hand, the study reinforced the typical bottom-line obstacles of time and effort required to host students. A trend was also noted related to gaps between educational preparation and clinical performance. Recent changes in the clinical environment were highlighted in the employer's responses, including the increasing use of technology in this workspace, along with more stringent regulation of the industry that affected student work.

As a result of the feedback, the analysis anticipated changes in clinical model that may include more focus on learning on-site and the need for longer clinical experiences. It was noted that the emerging practice of payment by educational institutions to cover employer's clinical education costs may also expand, due to the increasing numbers of AH programs and resulting competition for clinical sites. The main conclusion of the analysis of employer responses reinforced the criticality of collaboration between educators and employers, seen as essential to ensure that curriculum and outcomes match the needs of the field and effectively prepare students as entry-level clinicians.

Outside of the healthcare sector, study of the apprenticeship model has yielded the most information on benefit and costs. Research studies have examined Swiss and German companies, as these countries host the largest percentage of formal apprentice programs. Those studies generally showed a positive economic benefit, with the returns exceeding costs for employers.

Although research efforts to attempt to quantify the return on investment for companies who sponsor apprentices and participate in the RA model are limited in number, the methodologies used in recent studies have sought to answer some key questions; what motivates companies to initiate apprenticeship programs,[8] what analysis is used in the decision-making process to sustain such programs, and what were the bottom-line ROI metrics used by the companies to evaluate the practice?[9] These studies show multiple benefits which include an increase in employee retention, productivity gains during the employment of the apprentice, a positive return on the investment in the program and general satisfaction by those companies in the overall results of apprenticeship.

COMMON BENEFITS OF APPRENTICESHIP[10]

Production

- Output during the apprenticeship at a reduced wage
- Higher post-apprenticeship productivity relative to similarly tenured employees
- Reduction in mistakes or errors

Workforce

- Reduced turnover
- Better pipeline of skilled employees
- Better matching of employee skills and character with employer needs and company culture
- Lower recruiting costs
- Increased development of future managers

Soft Skills

- Higher employee engagement and loyalty
- Greater problem-solving ability and adaptability
- Reduced need for supervision

To better understand the perspective of sponsors, who are in most cases the employer, the United States Department of Labor's (USDOL) Education and Training Administration (ETA) commissioned a survey to learn more about what the outcomes of Registered Apprenticeship look like in the US (Lerman et al. 2009). Sponsoring companies were asked about characteristics of their program and about their views on the value, benefits, and drawbacks of registered apprenticeship, its integration with the workforce investment systems, apprentice completion and reasons for non-completion, and suggestions for possible improvement.[11]

In this study, 97 percent of sponsors of registered programs said they would recommend using the apprenticeship model to other firms. Of those companies, 86 percent stated they would "strongly" recommend it and the other 11 percent indicated they would recommend it with reservations, due primarily to problems with accessing related instruction.

The most frequently cited benefit of apprenticeship, identified as very important by over 80 percent of sponsors, was that it helped meet their demand for skilled workers. The second most frequently cited benefit was apprenticeship's role in reliably showing which workers have the skills needed. Other benefits, cited as very important, were: raising productivity, strengthening worker morale and pride, and improving worker safety. Most sponsors also cited the role of registered apprenticeship in worker recruitment and retention and in meeting licensing requirements.[12]

Drawbacks to the apprenticeship model identified by these companies are also important to note. The oft-cited issue of poaching, the fear of competitors taking away apprentices trained at the sponsor's cost, was shown as a concern but not a deterrent. Long thought by economists to be a major disincentive to employer involvement in apprenticeship, the results of this survey were a bit surprising. Only 25 percent of sponsors identified this as a significant problem while 29 percent saw it as a minor problem, and 46 percent did not perceive it as a problem at all. However, even among sponsors who perceived poaching as a problem, about 85 percent saw enough value in the practice and would still strongly recommend apprenticeship to others.

Retention of students in apprenticeship programs is an issue worldwide, with significant variability in program completion, ranging from above 90 percent in some programs to less than half in others. In the 2009 Lerman study, about a quarter of the sponsors viewed apprentices' failure to complete their apprenticeship program as a significant problem; 31 percent saw it as a minor problem and 45 percent did not cite it as a problem.

The most frequently cited reason for non-completion (by 36 percent of sponsors) was "personal issues" (family, health, legal, etc.). Performance problems on the job or in the classroom were the next most commonly cited reason (32 percent). Taking another job or transferring to another program was further down the list and less significant reasons for non-completion. Other studies indicate the quality of related technical instruction, lack of continuous employment (especially in the construction industry), length of the program, mentor/mentee relationship, and other factors as significant to the issue of apprentice retention. Only small percentages of sponsors in the DOLETA-sponsored study indicated they had significant problems with other aspects of an RA program, such as it taking too long to produce skilled workers, requiring too much effort to manage a program or too much paperwork involved.

Within this study, sponsors generally did not find costs to be a significant problem. Sixty-three percent of sponsors said related instruction costs were not a problem, although 30 percent viewed it as a minor problem and 6 percent as a major problem. Similarly, only 7 percent of respondents saw the costs of experienced workers' time to instruct apprentices as a significant problem, while 34 percent indicated it was a minor problem.[13]

In many of the research studies, the most-cited benefit of the RA model was reduced turnover—often considered more important than increased productivity.[14] Considering the costs and challenges of achieving a good "fit" between the potential employee and a specific company's culture, not to mention the ever-present possibility of a competitor poaching a trained employee, the bond created between the apprentice and the people in the workplace (both mentors and fellow apprentices) makes a strong case for the practice. Some companies stated that this loyalty factor (measured by attrition rate) makes employees more than twice as likely to stay with the company.[15]

Flexibility was also identified as a key advantage in these trainees. Given the fact that through related technical instruction, an apprentice is often well-versed in an understanding of the fundamental science and engineering principles related to the job. Thus they are sometimes more adept at problem-solving and more adaptable to new technologies than incumbent employees. In one case, apprentices could perform better on repair work that a company relied upon in its cyclical slack production time, and the ability to take on additional repair business thereby recouped an apprentice's overall training and employment cost within the first year.

Workforce professionals are responding to organizational changes in many of the companies we work with. Increasing competition in a global marketplace has forced many small to mid-size corporations, and even some large multinationals, to rethink their human resource function. Downsizing and budget cuts have played havoc with the training and development component of the HR departments in many companies.

Despite the significant constraints in the workforce pipeline, lacking this critical T&D function within HR has led to the general decline of corporate ability to define and implement a human resource development strategy.[16] Without a plan to address the workforce pipeline issue that includes a clear assessment of costs and benefits, firms are severely challenged in their decision-making capacity. It is important to note that although some costs or benefits can be very hard to measure, not including such measures ensures that their value is effectively zero.

It is also important to note that within this country, the advantage of RA program completion is clear—91 percent find employment after the apprenticeship, and the average starting wage is above $60,000.[17] On average, apprenticeship program completers earn $240,000 more during their entire career than nonparticipants.[18]

Among companies studied in this country, there is a general agreement that the model works. Value comes from both from the apprentice's productivity, which can reap economic returns above the cost of the program, as well as intrinsic factors like increased loyalty, creativity and expanded leadership potential. However, the net cost of apprenticeship programs varies widely across companies, and this variation exists across firms in other countries as well.[19] Some companies report that the cost is recouped very quickly, sometimes even during the apprenticeship period itself.[20]

Completion rates for apprenticeships are also highly variable - by country, by industry segment and by individual company. More research is needed to identify the causes of this inability to retain apprentices, as the cost of such efforts are often "sunk" early into corporate balance sheets for recruitment, program development and wages, and thus negatively affect the decision to continue to fund a work/learn strategy. A key finding of the extant research in sustaining a work-based learning program over time is to balance the interest of the employer, the apprentices, and the incumbent workforce.[21]

Workforce development departments at community colleges across the country work daily to assess, define and deliver worker training programs to the companies within their service regions. Often, these programs are highly focused on specific skills for either incumbent workers or to fill the jobs needed by their regional corporate customers. Our colleges generally do a good job at this task, and provide needed services to help address the obvious gaps. The workforce function at our colleges allows flexibility for delivery of these services, but sometimes those training solutions are not closely aligned or connected with the regular offerings of the colleges' academic and technical degree programs. Significant opportunity exists for growth within those credit-bearing programs when program leaders seek and support industry collaboration to ensure that curricular content is aligned with the RTI needs of regional firms.

Doing so, however, presents significant structural challenges within our institutions. Competent technical faculty are increasingly difficult to find, curricular change is time-consuming, and moving beyond the traditional program advisory committee format is a significant paradigm shift. Deeper engagement with corporate partners requires not only the realization that our students' employers are also key customers, but also demands significant staff time to develop and manage this new level of relationship.

Many technical programs with a successful WBL component have created corporate liaison roles akin to the clinical coordinator in the allied health discipline. This role can be a key determinant in the success of a program. The additional cost of such a position is often borne by the increased enrollment that is seen by programs that have a clear and direct pathway to family-sustaining employment.

HOW TO IMPLEMENT WORK-BASED LEARNING

Build Relationships

If apprenticeship and other WBL methods are all that effective, how do we convince companies to engage with us to implement such tactics? As we have noted, given the "push" system of education that has been in place in this country since its inception, companies may think it is the responsibility of government, state-sponsored education institutions and/or state workforce systems to supply trained workers. Companies may just not be positioned to develop a human resource development strategy. Operationalizing models that require sustained close collaboration with an educational provider requires time and effort. Presenting this type of solution requires a relationship of trust, a workable plan, and a bottom-line set of success indicators. Given the amount of pain that companies are experiencing around the workforce pipeline, it is now even more likely that these elements can be packaged into a convincing and consistent communication plan that helps us sell the idea of providing workplace applications for what we teach.

Use Labor Market Data

Workforce professionals may have developed good relationships with leaders within a company's HR or production departments, but selling a deeper engagement as well as a larger, sustained investment that is necessary for success in work-based learning will usually require involvement of C-suite executives. Data-driven decision-making is prevalent at this level of management, and we must be ready with data that supports the idea of work-based learning and shows a positive return on this critical investment.

The process we recommend must begin with good information, and any corporate executive, researcher or data analysis professional will know that data can be "massaged" to support differing opinions. In some states, more than one government entity gathers and reports on labor market data. Other states augment the official, rear-view-mirror reports with newer, internet-based real-time data sources. Those on the educational team must agree beforehand about whose data will be the basis for analysis and decision-making. Workforce professionals must be well-versed in the understanding and analysis of workforce supply-demand data, and be able to help companies both interpret, and even more importantly, validate the data based on local or regional market factors.

Define the Need

Leadership on the corporate side must perceive the business value in any solution and be able to quantify its expected results. Engagement is begun by reaching out and/or responding to the company, at which time we must ask appropriate questions to help clarify the workforce picture in terms more specific to the company's occupational needs, skills needed within those jobs, and the hiring projections over the short, mid-term and long-term time frames. Needs analysis is an important first-step skill for any practitioner and the process for this step of project development is addressed in other parts of this publication and its predecessors. Anyone working in this field must recognize that relationship development and maintenance is the essence of our work, and the time necessary for building good customer relationships must not be sacrificed to a cookie-cutter approach.

Tell the Story, State the Value

We must be ready with a strategy for the use of the data in decision-making, both to help with the marketing and communication of workable models for augmenting the workforce pipeline, and to frame that strategy with clear messages that will help businesses, workers, schools and students choose good paths and effective solutions. Connecting real, current data to a marketing and communication plan is essential in driving people to action.

It is important to remember that in everything we do, we are dealing with people, with the attendant emotional and behavioral factors that influence us all. Storytelling has been shown to be a powerful tool in helping people at all levels to relate to the impersonal data we are presenting. Personal stories of how work-based learning has affected peoples' lives and businesses, presented candidly and honestly, can be very effective in driving decisions by both employers and students. Stating the value of work-based learning starts with the research data on the ROI of apprenticeship and other work-based learning, which can be interpreted through stories of student and company success, and reinforced through examples of investments by companies across the globe in similar initiatives.

Practitioners have learned that for any workplace program or initiative to work and be sustainable it must be, first and foremost, driven by the company. Radically greater retention and graduation rates demonstrate the ability of employers to "pull" students through programs they have helped to define. This path to viable careers rivals our schools' collective ability to "push" students through college to an uncertain outcome.

Think Wholesale, not Retail

Workforce departments in today's college environment are stretched thin. Developing relationships with one company at a time, what has been termed as working "retail", continues to be an important part of building and maintaining our book of business. However, working "wholesale", or working with a larger group of businesses within a certain region or industry sector, can be a very effective way to use limited resources.

Engaging with a larger set of businesses to promote and expand work-based learning is admittedly more difficult than a one-business-at-a-time approach, so it is important to discuss the ways in which this might be accomplished. Sector-based work-and-learn strategies have been employed effectively in many regions to affect progress on workforce development, yet there are things to acknowledge as you consider such a strategy.

Given the multitude of potential stakeholders within a larger set of companies, you should first give thought to describing the sector. Identifying which companies you should reach out to, and where the leaders and influencers are in a particular region or sector is an important first step. You should also think about the other stakeholders in this landscape.

Are there strong leaders in industry sector associations, local or regional economic development organizations, or other government agencies that have built relationships with these companies and who can contribute value to the effort? Who among these stakeholders might have the best influence to convene the companies that you think may have a mutual interest in participating in a work/learn model? The role of convener is a key one in beginning and sustaining this effort.

Consider a Convener

There are research findings that indicate that a neutral, third-party entity with experience in building workforce collaboratives can be an effective convener for such work.[22] An intermediary that has a reputation for success in this arena and ability to quickly build trust can be effective in getting the right people around the table. Finding such a partner will not always be easy, but an experienced team can navigate and help mitigate the multiple barriers between education and industry to accelerate the progress of a sector initiative.

Consider if a third party will add real value to initiating and sustaining the project. Oftentimes there may be a local or regional organization that has experience in this work that can be engaged in an initial convener role that evolves into a project management role. Be cognizant that part of the work is change management, and organizations with a history of preparing groups for disruption and change can also be effective.

The criticality of industry leadership in any such sector-based effort cannot be overstated. If companies step up to provide effective leadership for convening, needs analysis, work/learn model development and implementation, there may not need to be third-party involvement. Remember that the more parties that are involved in any project, the number of communication channels expand exponentially.

Emphasize Partnership

Industry leaders can be convinced that they are a key partner by thoughtful and inclusive engagement of the education organization. Business and industry leaders may have a long-held belief that government, through its provision of K–12, public higher education and various workforce programs, has the sole responsibility for making sure that the general population has the right skills to be successful in the workplace. They have been reinforced in this thinking over time by generally being marginalized in the policy and practice of education. The pain that these companies experience today provides an opening for the reexamination of that belief. This will not happen, however, without educational practitioners' willingness to genuinely listen to industry leaders, work closely and diligently with them, and then modify the content and delivery of our educational programs.

Experiential learning programs must be designed and implemented with a great deal of thought toward the role of program management. Traditional college instruction is guided by college policy and course syllabi, yet the management and day-to day delivery of the program is placed mostly in the hands of faculty, with oversight by deans and other administrators. Expanding the place of learning from the classroom and lab into a business office, factory floor or other jobsite can exponentially complicate the management of student learning.

Just sending a student out to a company location for "experience" is not effective educational practice and does not use either the student's or company's resources to full learning effect. Relying on the devotion of the apprentice or minimizing the influence of the workplace mentor is not good practice, nor is happenstance a timely teacher.

History provides many examples of how the master/apprentice relationship has been managed, for good or ill. In the old days, the disciple might have been assigned menial or less productive work to gauge his/her devotion and dedication. The master demonstrated skills within daily work. The apprentice was sometimes expected to glean knowledge and skill organically by noticing and then seeking a chance to apply the practice. In recent times, companies have used interns to fill temporary or menial roles, not connected to the educational goals of the student. Neither transmits knowledge and skills at a pace needed in today's rapidly evolving business environment. Managing how a student is applying, at the workplace setting, the theory or skills currently being presented in the college course is a critical issue as we discuss how best to utilize this proven practice for the integration of education and work.

Focus on Communication

The integration of theory and practice through experiential learning requires a much higher level of communication between the industry and educational partners. Ideally, through planning and collaborative content development, each partner has contributed time and effort to the process, prior to any student arriving at a company site. Effective work-based learning programs also consider the connection between the faculty and the student's supervisor at work. Communication between these teacher/mentor roles is absolutely necessary. Each has an influence on the student's learning progress, so each must understand the objectives of the current coursework and the individual student's status within the learning progression.

Faculty are an essential and central piece of any experiential learning process. First and foremost, faculty must understand that their role in higher education is not threatened or marginalized in adopting a greater connection to the careers that their students will ultimately gain. They must recognize the drivers of change from an economic perspective—not only the previously-discussed change in the perception of the value of higher education by the public, but also the economic development factors that prevent those potential students from filling the seats in their dwindling classrooms.

Technical program faculty may be more comfortable in moving toward work-based learning strategies, but the traditional liberal arts faculty can benefit significantly from the constant clamor in the business sector for employability or soft skills—especially the "4 C's"—communication, collaboration, critical thinking and creativity—as these are precisely the skills that they seek to impart to their students through the intellectual development at the heart of their coursework. Unfreezing attitudes is said to be the first step of change in any practice, and the economic realities can help faculty thaw their thinking about the products produced by higher education in today's landscape.

Faculty must understand that experiential learning is not another "add-on"; it is an essential change in the way education can be facilitated. Confronted with doing more with less, faculty must decide to work smarter, not harder.

Faced with all the other pressures of shrinking budgets, smaller enrollments, increased expectations and the "adjunctification" of the teaching practice, faculty can see a deeply engaged business partner as either a threat or a helping hand. Hopefully, the latter offer will be accepted. Many examples now exist that can show faculty that the initial work developing and building relationships with a business for the benefit of students is one that pays off in productive and transformative ways. Good work-based learning programs actually make it easier for faculty to do their job. It allows them to move from a labor-intensive role as the sole source of knowledge delivery to one that collaboratively facilitates the transfer and application of knowledge.

Many faculty members have taken up a teaching role because at the core, their belief system and personal reward includes providing service to students. Student success is a value often held and stated by faculty as an argument for maintaining the status quo in the practice of teaching. This core value can be used as an effective argument for change. Stories of student success, from credentials earned without debt, to direct pathways to well-paid careers, are powerful tools to motivate faculty to incorporate WBL in their programs.

Use a "Boundary Spanner"

Faculty can benefit from another essential part of any functional work-based learning strategy—that of the business liaison. This essential role is a central part of the overall management of successful work/learn programs. The liaison functions as a key customer relationship manager, working closely with the student, the company at which they are placed, and the faculty that teaches within the program. Given the previously-stated constraints upon faculty time and effort, the liaison serves as a "boundary spanner"—facilitating and maintaining the corporate relationship so that faculty can do what they do best—manage student learning. Liaisons don't replace that needed interaction; they simply enhance the communication between faculty and corporate staff.

In work/learn programs proven to be successful, the workplace learning liaison role is key and includes multiple functions. This person is often the primary relationship manager between the college and the company. They are often involved with potential students early on in the process, helping manage recruitment, evaluation and placement activities on both sides of the partnership. The liaison serves as the main contact for the student with the typical college student services—enrollment, registration, financial aid, advisement, etc.

In some cases, the "success coach" also helps students through much more personal challenges—the things we know that are often the main reasons why students do not persist—family issues, getting to work, and other non-academic challenges. Their closer relationship to the student may position them to know when the student is at risk of not succeeding in the program, and this closer interaction can facilitate solutions to a range of problems.

Through regular, deep and honest engagement with a sponsoring company, the liaison builds integrity and trust; essential ingredients in any work/learn partnership. They communicate openly and consistently with company representatives, faculty and other college personnel to ensure that channels remain open and issues are identified and resolved. This unique and emerging role ensures both student success and the success of the partnership.

Don't Neglect the Mentor

Another element that must be addressed in any work-based learning design is the role of the on-site mentor. Traditional education is focused on defining and delivering specified learning goals, outcomes and performance objectives. The role of faculty is well-defined in standard educational practice. For programs that have an experiential component, thought must be given to how the on-site mentor functions to achieve the applied learning goals of the program. Not just any employee can effectively function as a mentor, and the research literature shows that the mentor/mentee relationship is an important determinant of student retention and success.

The transfer of knowledge from mentor to mentee is a key component of any work-based learning. It is too important to leave this element to chance. Collaborative thought must thus be given to the selection and development of the workplace mentor. This role is not solely one of supervisor, as it encompasses the larger task of learning facilitation, often in a one-on-one or small group format. In the ideal environment, learning is accomplished not only by the student, but also by the faculty and the mentor.

CONCLUSION

It is an old adage that people are a company's most important asset. But in today's knowledge-based economy, it is the knowledge in the heads of those employees that is the real asset. Many mature companies understand that they are in the business of selling knowledge, and some recognize that their real product is the knowledge that resides in the corporate body. For some time, progressive corporate leaders have been focused on the activity of knowledge management; striving to elicit, document, and transfer that knowledge to those that will carry on the work of the company.

Practitioners in the field of knowledge management understand that it is much easier to do so with explicit forms of knowledge (tasks, methods and procedures) than the tacit forms of knowledge that subject matter experts have developed for ways of doing things within the company. This tacit knowledge, knowing who and where to go to for information and action, is also critical for companies to transfer to new employees. Transfer of tacit knowledge requires extensive personal contact and communication. For work-based learning programs, it is important to build explicit linkages between the college program and the person(s) that directly impact students in the workplace, in order to facilitate this transfer of both explicit and tacit knowledge.[23]

Many companies now understand that work-based learning, combined with subsequent employment, is a good strategy for knowledge management, since it will ensure that those assets will remain within and benefit the company in the long term.

Another key element of work-based learning is the recruitment of talent into the pipeline. Like other facets of this process, the responsibility for finding students is not solely that of one of the partners. Successfully attracting the right students into a program with a work requirement necessitates the integration of the college and employers in the marketing and recruitment effort.

The challenge for both is to attract qualified candidates—those that have the greatest potential for completion and ultimately a good fit for the job. To do this, colleges cannot simply sell their programs, and companies cannot simply offer entry-level employment, as they have in the past. Successful marketing and recruiting efforts leverage the power of both partners, with recruiters from both college and company working arm in arm to execute a deliberate student recruitment strategy.

In higher education, matching and engaging a potential student with a particular training program has to date been the realm of college advisors and career counselors. Neither of these functions has typically been well funded or coordinated. This essential matching function is one that has now been taken up by some third-party organizations, providing a service on the front end of workplace learning programs. This matching role has been shown as an integral factor in the rapid growth of apprenticeship programs in the United Kingdom. This nascent effort is not yet widespread in the United States, but may be helpful in reaching out into specific communities to promote, connect, and match potential candidates with the right opportunity.

Strategic thinking and planning is also necessary to identify the qualities needed in the workforce and then determine how program candidates can be assessed and selected in order to meet the employer's talent needs, while advancing corporate ethical standards of access and inclusion. Especially in hire-first programs, the college and company must agree upon candidate selection standards and process, and then follow those religiously.

Likewise, both of these partners must agree upon and uphold student/employee performance standards. In the best programs, college and company together reinforce the need for a high level of performance in both the classroom and in the workplace. Too much effort and too many resources are invested to be negligent in monitoring day-to-day student performance. Those programs that maintain a close connection to students and address the inevitable problems that arise, either at work or at home, are the ones that achieve high completion and subsequent employment rates. Like most other things in life, communication is the key, and it is incumbent upon all of the players on this stage - the faculty, the college and company liaisons, the workplace mentor, and the student - to maintain open communication channels.

As workforce development professionals, it is incumbent upon us to continue to research and learn about methods of experiential learning, and apply that knowledge to appropriate situations within our own practice. As a community of practice, we need increase our advocacy and drive a discussion about this topic, in order to achieve progress on the shortcomings that limit knowledge and growth:

- Agreement on a common definition of work-based learning,
- Development of a widely-used forum to share best practices in this arena,
- Dissemination of strategies to scale up programs that are proven to work, and
- A common platform upon which to share data in regard to work-based learning

No doubt, the process of learning while working will continue to be a method for increasing the effectiveness of education, as it has been proven over time to be quite useful. Progress on the above four points will allow this learning methodology to be improved and practiced more widely. It is certainly not the only tool in our toolbox, but it is one that has garnered more attention in recent years. It can be expanded to benefit our institutions, our corporate customers, and most of all, our students.

BEST PRACTICES IN WORK-BASED LEARNING

Build Relationships

Spend less time in the office and more out in the field, meeting with clients and potential clients. Use a customer relationship management (CRM) system to identify and qualify potential clients and track project activity.

Use Labor Market Data

An important part of your job is knowing the delta between your college's programming and its outcomes, in comparison to the demand in your region's workforce marketplace. Can you easily access and analyze that data at your college? Some state systems already have robust tools, sophisticated longitudinal datasets, and staff that can help you to know the landscape. Make sure that real-time data is included in your regional labor market analysis.

The US Chamber of Commerce has begun a new initiative to assist in this work. Its Talent Pipeline Academy is designed to provide structure, guidance and tools that groups of companies can utilize to validate the regional supply/demand information and plan strategic actions to ensure the talent pipeline development efforts are appropriate for the group. Similarly, the National Governors Association is engaged in a Good Jobs for All Americans initiative, and your state may be participating in that effort.

Define the Need

When defining and analyzing needs, ask the standard questions and then *listen*. Document what you are hearing, without preconceptions. You may think you have heard it all before, and that this company is no different than many you have worked with in the past. Everyone is struggling to find employees, are they not? By using active listening techniques, you may find an issue or situation that offers a unique solution. Don't just sell the product on the shelf (existing program X or Y). Listen to their perception of the problem. Continue to ask the "why" question to dig for the root cause.

Tell the Story, State the Value

Personalize the data by using student success stories, drawing from aspirations common to all of us. Make sure that you gain permission to publicize these powerful statements. Don't forget the corporate perspective, which can be used to demonstrate and encourage WBL implementation by other companies.

Think Wholesale, Not Retail

Use a specific company's success with WBL to drive workplace learning programs throughout its own supply chain. The peer-to-peer relationship that is already present between these trading partners helps other companies to emulate success rather than assume all the risks in innovation and implementation of a new, untested program. A mentoring relationship can be established between the company with experience with the program and the new company. Such mentoring has been shown effective in rapidly accelerating implementation and success.

The FAME model (Federation of Advanced Manufacturing Excellence) is an example of this strategy that began with Toyota Motor Manufacturing in the state of Kentucky and has now spread throughout the country and to other industry sectors as well. This work/learn model was designed by Toyota in partnership with its local community college and then expanded through its automotive supply chain. College classes and paid experience in the workplace ensures full-time student engagement and on-the-job application of advanced manufacturing theory and skill. FAME is based on a regional "chapter" structure with company leadership driving the recruitment, student employment and management of the individual chapters.

Consider a Convener

Identify who's driving the bus. That could potentially be a third party at the outset. Remember, leadership can sometimes be most effective from a position in the middle. When gathering a broad set of stakeholders, perceived roles are important. Initially, you may be perceived as a vendor with your own agenda rather than an impartial convener. Once progress and trust are established, the group may evolve to provide its own leadership team.

Emphasize Partnership

Strive to work closely and diligently with industry leaders, with full awareness of shared risks and benefits. Be willing to do the hard work necessary to modify the content, delivery and management of your educational programs.

Focus on Communication that Drives Results

Create a communication plan. Agree upon a standard assessment, tied to the goals and objectives of the educational program, which will be used by the supervisor/mentor during the student's activity at the company site. This should include a gauge of the student's progress on specific psychomotor and affective learning outcomes. Plan a timetable to use this assessment for regular feedback from company representative to faculty. This can be an effective communication channel that will minimize, but not replace, face-to-face interaction between the students' learning partners. The reality of shift work, distance and time can severely hamper the communication between faculty and mentor, yet each must be apprised of student performance status (and potential countervailing issues) in order to provide the best guidance for expected learning.

Use a "Boundary Spanner"

Sometimes called a "success coach" or other similar title, a college staff person in the role of workplace liaison functions as a key customer relationship manager, working closely with the student, the company at which they are placed, and the faculty that teaches within the program. Given the significant constraints upon faculty time and effort, the liaison serves as a "boundary spanner" - facilitating and maintaining the corporate relationship so that faculty can do what they do best—manage student learning. Liaisons don't replace that needed interaction; they simply enhance the communication between faculty and corporate staff.

Don't Neglect the Mentor

The person(s) that interact with students in the workplace are the most important part of the WBL, so don't take this element for granted. Not everyone that knows how to do something can teach it to someone else. Incorporate mentor assessment and development into any WBL program. The student is not the only benefactor of this approach. Research shows that this role can be a powerful morale booster and retention factor for company staff that work with students.

NOTES

1. Helper, S., Noonan, R., Nicholson, J., and Langdon, D. (2016). *The benefits and costs of apprenticeship: A business perspective.* Case Western Reserve University & U.S. Department of Commerce, Economics and Statistics Administration, Office of the Chief Economist.

2. Ladyshewsky, R., Barrie, S., and Drake, V. (1998). *A comparison of productivity and learning outcome in individual and cooperative physical therapy clinical education models.* Physical Therapy; 78(12): 1288–98.

3. Phelan, S., Daniels, M., and Hewitt, L. (1999). *The costs and benefits of clinical education.* Laboratory Medicine; 30(11): 714–20.

4. Meyers, S. (1995). *Exploring the costs and benefits drivers of clinical education.* American Journal of Occupational Therapy; 49(2): 107–11.

5. Chung, Y., Spelbring, L., and Boissoneau, R. (1980). *A cost-benefit analysis of fieldwork education in occupational therapy.* Inquiry; 17(3): 216–29.

6. Dizon, J., Grimmer-Somers, K., and Kumar, S. (2012). *Current evidence on evidence-based practice training in allied health: A systematic review of the literature.* International Journal of Evidence-Based Healthcare; 10: 347–60.

7. O'Brien, C., Anderson, R., Ayzenberg, B., et al. (2017). *Employers' viewpoint on clinical education*. Journal of Allied Health; 46(3): 131–37. Available at: https://static1.squarespace.com/static/57a64a023e00beb95af13929/t/5a09b86153450af07ce55812/1510586466048/Employers percent27+Viewpoint+on+Clinical+Education.pdf

8. Helper, S., Noonan, R., Nicholson, J., and Langdon, D. (2016). *The benefits and costs of apprenticeship: A business perspective*. Case Western Reserve University & U.S. Department of Commerce, Economics and Statistics Administration, Office of the Chief Economist.

9. Lerman, R., (2014). *Do firms benefit from apprenticeship investments?* IZA World of Labor. Available at: http://wol.iza.org/articles/do-firms-benefit-from-apprenticeship-investments.pdf

10. Helper, S., et al, (2016). *The benefits and costs of apprenticeship: A business perspective*, pg. 23.

11. Lerman, R., Eyster, L., and Chambers, K. (2009). The benefits and challenges of registered apprenticeship: The sponsors' perspective. Urban Institute. Available at: https://www.urban.org/research/publication/benefits-and-challenges-registered-apprenticeship-sponsors-perspective.

12. Ibid, pg. ii.

13. Ibid, pg. ii.

14. Helper, S., et al, (2016). *The benefits and costs of apprenticeship: A business perspective*, pg. 23.

15. In the Helper Study, CVS Health officials stated that apprenticeship participation doubled the likeliness of that employee to stay with the company. Blue Cross/Blue Shield of South Carolina cited an attrition rate of 4 percent, compared with an industry average of 13 percent. Dartmouth-Hitchcock noted that the program also affected a reduction in turnover for other employees.

16. Society for Human Resource Management (SHRM). (2015). *Practicing strategic human resources*. Available at: https://www.shrm.org/resourcesandtools/tools-and-samples/toolkits/pages/practicingstrategichumanresources.aspx

17. Perez, T., and Zients, J. *ApprenticeshipUSA is upskilling america*. Department of Labor Blog. October 21, 2016. Available at: https://blog.dol.gov/2016/10/21/apprenticeshipusa-is-upskilling-america/.

18. Reed, D., Yung-Hsu Liu, A., Klienman, R., Mastri, A., Reed, D., Sattar, S., and Ziegler, J. (2012). *An effectiveness assessment and cost-benefit analysis of registered apprenticeship in 10 states*. Mathematica Policy Research. Available at: https://wdr.doleta.gov/research/FullText_Documents/ETAOP_2012_10.pdf.

19. Muehlemann, S., and Wolter, S., (November 2014). *Return on investment of apprenticeship systems for enterprises: Evidence from cost-benefit analyses*. IZA Journal of Labor Policy, 03:25. Available at: https://izajolp.springeropen.com/articles/10.1186/2193-9004-3-25.

20. Mohrenweiser, J., and Zwick, T. (2008). *Why do firms train apprentices? The net cost puzzle reconsidered*. Center for European Economic Research, Discussion Paper 08-019. Available at: ftp://ftp.zew.de/pub/zew-docs/dp/dp08019.pdf.

21. Helper, S., et al, (2016), pg. 3.

22. Prince, H., King, C., and Oldmixon, S. (2017) *Promoting the adoption of sector strategies by workforce development boards under the workforce innovation and opportunity act*. University of Texas, Austin, TX. Available at: https://raymarshallcenter.org/files/2017/05/Sector_Strategy_Final_Report_March_2017.pdf

23. Davenport, T., and Prusak, L. (1998). *Working knowledge: How organizations manage what they know*. Harvard Business School Press, Boston, MA.

Chapter Eleven

Finance and Budgeting for Workforce Professionals

John Will

Workforce development professionals play a critical role in helping people develop the skills needed to effectively function in the labor market. Training is specifically designed to align with jobs that satisfy individual interests and that will lead to gainful employment. Successful programming also provides value to employers and consumers. Employers are served when the economy is supplied with the necessary workers to meet labor market demand, which in turn helps consumers by ensuring quality products or services are available.

When considering the critical role of workforce development organizations in supporting the overall economic well-being of a service area or region, the importance of Finance and Budgeting processes quickly becomes apparent. Allocating and managing resources effectively will literally make or break an organization's effort to support the local economy and its various stakeholder groups. As such, the Finance and Budgeting processes intersect with the most important policy and strategic decisions of any workforce development organization, and it is the workforce development professional's responsibility to understand how they work.

The following sections are designed to provide a brief step-by-step overview of what to consider when learning about the Finance and Budgeting processes in a typical workforce development operation.

STEP 1: UNDERSTAND THE MARKET

Before beginning the process of creating a budget or reading a financial statement, workforce development professionals should develop an understanding of the labor market. Normally, there are circumstances that will inform subsequent finance and budgeting decisions. Often these will be reflected in easy-to-obtain information. For example, the unemployment rate, labor participation rate, and per capita income are likely readily available from public sources. Information related to population characteristics, such as age and educational attainment levels, could also be helpful. Supplementing this kind of data with feedback from stakeholders, such as major employers or economic development colleagues, will help determine priorities as the finance and budgeting processes take shape.

To help explain why Step 1 is important, consider the characteristics of two simple labor markets as described below (see table 11.1).

The task of developing an understanding of the labor market is complex, but even with these simple variables it is evident that the strategies supported by finance and budgeting decisions will vary based on market conditions. It is helpful to think of the budget as a "reflection" of priorities rather than a "direction." It is easy to see why the workforce development organization operating in Labor Market 1 would likely try to reflect programming that helped people find entry-level positions.

Language classes may need to be a component or providing the instruction in a different language may be an option. For Labor Market 2, the considerations are clearly different. Programming would ideally reflect the needs of incumbent workers who lack the skills necessary to be promoted into better jobs. It is possible private entities would contract for services for incumbent workers.

Regardless of the solutions that are ultimately proposed, it's clear that a workforce development professional needs to know his or her market before

Table 11.1. Considering the Characteristics of Two Simple Labor Markets

	Labor Market 1	Labor Market 2
Unemployment rate	8%	3%
Labor participation rate	55%	68%
Post-secondary educational attainment	37%	56%
Average age	49	38
Largest employer	ABC Precision Machining	MapleLeaf Medical Center
Chamber of Commerce Comment	"Employers want to hire, but a key challenge is that our large immigrant community is challenged by a language barrier."	"Professional development at night or online would help get people into better jobs. It seems like everyone has a job so there is no time to go to school."

making important resource allocation decisions. Collecting basic information that at least partially describes the characteristics of the workforce will help with decision-making later.

STEP 2: KNOW THE FINANCIAL STATEMENTS

Before learning about an organization's financial operation, it is important to know that in most organizations a general understanding of the three basic financial statements will be necessary. Although alternative titles are sometimes used, these include the Income Statement, Balance Sheet, and Statement of Cash Flows. A complete set of all three basic financial statements are prepared relatively infrequently.

For example, in many government organizations the full financial statements may only be prepared after the end of the year for the purposes of having them audited by a public accountant. Periodic management reports often contain components of the basic financial statements and it is critical to have a sense of how they are used and how they are connected to the three basic financial statements.

The Income Statement

In private organizations, the Income Statement (or Profit and Loss), explains how resources are generated in the form of revenues and how they are used in the form of expenses. In governmental entities the equivalent information is provided but is often called the Statement of Activities. The basic measurement to consider is whether sources of revenues exceed uses of funding, or expenditures.

Private organizations likely have established profit expectations where revenues exceed expenditures, while governmental entities may simply seek to break even. Unless there are unusual circumstances a loss caused by insufficient revenue will signal a problem. Some public workforce development operations may receive support through taxing authority, governmental support like state aid, or federal grants that allow them to operate at a level where the revenue collected for services rendered is less than the cost of those services.

A simple Income Statement is provided below as an example:

Workforce Solutions
Income Statement
June 30, 20XX
Revenue
Training contract revenue $323,000

Seminar fees		74,200
Interest income		2,200
Total revenue		$399,400
Expenses		
	Wages and benefits	$274,000
	Training supplies	55,000
	Equipment lease	27,000
	Interest expense	5,000
Marketing expense		5,000
Depreciation		6,000
	Total expense	$372,000
Net Income		$ 27,400

Depending on the type of organization, sometimes overhead costs like administrative salaries will be broken out separately from costs that are directly associated with services provided. However, the basic concept of finding the difference between revenues generated and expenses incurred to determine net income will be reflected in any income statement. In this specific example, Workforce Solutions generates net income of $27,400, a figure that will show up again in the sample financial statements.

The income statement measures financial activity over a period, often for one month or one year. It represents a summary of transactions from a start date to and end date.

The Balance Sheet

The next financial statement important to understand is the Balance Sheet, or in governmental entities Statement of Net Position. This financial statement summarizes the workforce development organization's assets, liabilities, and equity. Assets include things that are owned, like buildings, cash in bank accounts, investments, and equipment. Liabilities include things that are owed, like loans from banks or accounts payable to vendors. When assets exceed liabilities the organization has Equity, or in the case of governments, a positive Net Position. The basic measurement to look for on this financial statement is Equity or Net Position. If the number is negative, the organization may not be solvent.

It's important to note that workforce development organizations often require modern equipment to meet the needs of business and industry. If assets attributed to the workforce development operation are minimal or are fully depreciated it could indicate a need a need to invest in or update equipment, even if the positive Equity or Net Assets appears in on the Balance

Sheet. This information can also be found by closely reviewing the Balance Sheet.

A simple example of a Balance Sheet is provided below:

Workforce Solutions
Balance Sheet
June 30, 20XX

Assets

	Cash	$40,000
	Training contracts receivable	40,000
	Equipment, less accumulated depreciation of $120,000	37,200
	Total assets	$117,200

Liabilities and Equity

	Payroll liabilities	$12,500
	Note payable	80,000
	Total liabilities	$92,500
Equity (1)		$24,700
Total Liabilities and Equity		$117,200

Equity increased through the generation of net income; no distributions to or contributions from owners impacted equity in the reporting period.

A basic principal of accounting is that assets always equal liabilities plus equity. In this example, Workforce Solutions has positive equity of $24,700. Given that net income increases equity and no other transactions affected equity, it appears based on the information we have that net income substantially improved the equity position of Workforce Resources in the reporting period. In addition, the depreciation information suggests that the equipment owned is somewhat old with a large accumulated depreciation of balance $120,000 relative to the net reported value of $37,000.

The balance sheet represents an organizations financial position at a specific point in time. Think of it as a 'snapshot' of everything that is owned and owed as of a specific date.

The Statement of Cash Flows

Finally, the third financial statement to consider assesses cash flow. This is often the least intuitive of the financial statements, but a basic understanding of how cash flows in and out of any organization is vital. Like any enterprise, workforce development organizations need cash to operate. Often services are provided before payment is received, so a beginning positive cash balance is critical. Like the income statement, the Statement of Cash Flows measures activity for a specific period with a specific focus on how cash is generated and used.

Generally, a healthy workforce development organization will generate cash from its operations unless there is a planned subsidy from a public or private source. This basic measure suggests that services are being provided above cost and that the payment is being collected from customers, who are usually students or a sponsor, like an employer. A workforce development organization that generates cash from operations can use it as a cushion to avoid borrowing to meet basic obligations, such as vendor payments. It can also consider financing asset purchases or reducing debt with surplus cash. In for-profit organizations, cash can be distributed back to owners as a return on their investment.

Cash can also be generated from financing or investing activities. In most workforce development entities, issuing debt is the most common vehicle for generating cash in this manner. Debt is normally used to acquire assets that will improve operating cash flow (e.g., equipment that can be used to provide more services that generate cash from operations). If debt is regularly used to buy assets that do not improve cash flow (and net income) the organization will eventually run out of cash, be unable to pay its debts, and will reduce its equity.

A simple example of a Statement of Cash Flows is provided below:

Workforce Solutions
Statement of Cash Flows
June 30, 20XX

Operating activities		
Net Income		$27,400
	Increase (decrease) in training contracts receivable	(11,000)
	Depreciation	6,000
	Cash generated from operations	$22,400
Financing activities		
	Decrease in notes payable	($10,000)
Change in cash for the reporting period		$12,400
Beginning cash		$27,600
Ending cash		$40,000

One key takeaway from this example is that cash from operations was less than net income. This occurs because there is an increase in receivables, which means a customer owes Workforce Solutions money. Depreciation does not use cash, so it gets added back. In addition, payments were made on a note that used cash.

A second takeaway is that the basic financial statements are connected. Net income, which represents a summary of all the revenue and expenses, appears on both the Income Statement and Statement of Cash Flows. Cash appears on both the Balance Sheet and Statement of Cash Flows, as do changes in other asset and liability accounts. While it is beyond the scope of this chapter to explain these connections in detail, know that each financial statement reports a different, but connected, measure of financial health. For Workforce Solutions, a reasonable assessment for the reporting period is that it is a profitable organization (see Income Statement) with an improving financial position (see Balance Sheet, and the increase in equity), and solid cash flow that is being used in part to pay down debt (see Statement of Cash Flows). Growing receivables and the age of the equipment may be areas to learn more about.

Beyond the Financial Statements

For workforce development organizations that receive direct public support, such as state aid, or who receive indirect support, such as grants through the Department of Labor, linking performance measures to resource allocation decisions has become more important with the advent of the accountability movement. These measurements will deepen the understanding of the market and the Finance and Budgeting processes. For example, job placement and graduate (or completer) starting pay are common measures that are considered to evaluate the effective use of resource allocations in a workforce development organization.

A very sophisticated workforce development organization will take financial and non-financial measurement further by benchmarking against other organizations. Taking the time to consider how one organization compares to another can open the door to discussions about opportunities and challenges that could not emerge with even the most in-depth and expert understanding of the financial statements in isolation.

STEP 3: UNDERSTAND THE BUDGET DOCUMENTS

Various financial reports are a critical tool in assessing the effectiveness and sustainability in workforce development efforts. Once key market considerations are identified it will be important to understand the documents that have been used to develop and monitor the organization's financial plan. A budget document will be available prior to the start of the year and represents management's best estimate of how it will generate and use the resources of the workforce development organization. This document will highlight *expected* sources of revenue and expenses, which is normally presented in a format like an Income Statement. The budget document explains what decision-makers *think* will happen, and in that sense represents a projection or best guess.

Budgets are a key tool for creating expectations and accountability to the financial plan. For larger organizations, a projected Balance Sheet and Statement of Cash Flows is often provided as well. For workforce development operations that are the sole focus of the organization, such as a non-profit workforce development board, the budget information may come in the form of an adopted budget document approved by a governing board.

For workforce development operations that represent a department within a larger organization, like a university or college, more specific reports from a central finance office may be pertinent. While the entire organization's budget will certainly be useful to know, a department level budget formatted much like an income statement will be available and it will be focused on specific workforce development activities.

A complete Balance Sheet and Statement of Cash Flows probably will not be prepared at the department level, but the operations of the department will certainly impact the broader financial statements. Understanding this impact can be important when advocating for strategic, policy, or resource allocation decisions. Whether working with an organization-level budget document or department-level reports, seeing a snapshot of the financial plan in the form of a budget is an excellent place to develop an overall understanding how resources are expected to flow in and out of the organization.

STEP 4: MONITOR THE OPERATION

Of the three primary financial statements, the one most often used for periodic monitoring is a version of the Income Statement. Unlike initial budget documents, monitoring reports include a comparison of budgeted amounts to actual spending as of a certain report date. Detailed budget reports are often available by department or manager or both.

Monthly monitoring by leadership or a supervisor is common, but more frequent reporting may be appropriate. Supplemental information such as how spending compares to the prior year at the same point, cash and investment balances, or major financing activities may also be included. These reports are also an excellent starting point for developing subsequent budgets.

For many organizations, an annual audit will be performed by an independent accounting firm. Audits review a sample of the activities for a prior reporting period (usually a year), include all three financial statements, and provide a myriad of notes and other supplemental information. The report helps leaders and other stakeholders ensure that reasonable processes are in place and that accounting practices are in line with common standards.

The primary purpose of the auditor is simply to evaluate whether the financial statements reflect an accurate portrayal of financial activities. An auditor will render an "unmodified" opinion if the financial statements are presented in accordance with applicable auditing standards. Other opinions indicate a deficiency and will be accompanied by further explanation from the auditor.

Auditors and audit reports can also highlight major concerns about an organization's performance, such as a recurring pattern of losses or issues related to grant compliance. If the management of the workforce development organization communicates the plan through the budget and monitoring reports throughout the year, the audit report should not present surprises. However, if activities create recurring losses or deviate from the broader organization's policies, it is possible the auditor will raise concerns or identify opportunities for improvement.

An important distinction between budget documents and audit documents is their timing. A budget document represents a plan and is thus forward looking.

Periodic reporting during the year shows how actual activities stack up as compared to the plan, and sometimes it is necessary to modify the budget as a result. In contrast, the audit is generally backward looking. It is sometimes referred to as "autopsy" information to reflect that outcomes in the report can no longer be changed. While it is important and useful, most workforce development professionals will spend most of their energy developing and implementing the budget and financing plans.

ADOPTING A CONTINUOUS IMPROVEMENT MINDSET

An introduction to finance and budgeting in a workforce development organization would be incomplete without mention of the importance of adopting a continuous improvement mindset. Workforce development organizations are focused on a collection of processes that lead to very specific outcomes, those that are related to training connected to employment. These processes are often the focus of resource allocation decisions, which ultimately lead to success or failure when measured against desired results.

Combined with an understanding of financial and non-financial measures, it follows that understanding these processes and continually working to make them better will improve educational and training outcomes through more effective finance and budgeting decisions. For example, a great training process with a bureaucratic, inefficient registration process won't maximize results. Continuous improvement efforts focus on reducing "waste," or the aspects processes that do not add value. In the example provided, eliminating any unnecessary steps from the registration process would be a simple continuous improvement activity. Even when organizations are effective, it is important to continually seek to improve the processes that support that success.

This chapter provided a brief summary of the basic financial statements and other, major considerations related to finance and budgeting in workforce development organizations. Given the importance of workforce development efforts to students, employers, and consumers, it is critical to understand how the financial operation intersects with strategic and operational decision making. The following sections summarize the key lessons learned and the competencies that should have been developed based on the chapter's content.

CONCLUSION

Don't start with the finances. Rather, develop an understanding of the market being served and be prepared to connect this knowledge with what you learn about the financial plan or budget.

It's not necessary to be an accountant to understand the financial statements. From budget development to periodic monitoring to the final audit, the financial statements represent the "language" that is used to discuss expectations and accountability for the financial aspects of the organization. Speaking the language is critical when articulating the value of the workforce development operation.

- Where possible, try to compare financial and non-financial measures to other similar organizations to see if gaps exist.
- Read the available budget documents. Knowing organizational and, if applicable, departmental expectations will be critical when making resource allocation and other policy-based decisions. The more you know about the budget, the better.
- Monitor financial activities by comparing actual performance to the budget on a regular basis. Adjustments to the plan may be an option if they are identified during the year.
- Read the audit report with the understanding it is "autopsy" information. If possible, find out what the auditor has to say about opportunities for improvement and be constructive in offering solutions through the appropriate channels.
- Consider non-financial measures of performance and how they relate to Finance and Budgeting decisions. Make sure that financial decisions are in alignment with the non-financial mission or goals of the organization.
- Work towards adopting a continuous improvement mindset when making finance and budgeting decisions.

- Above all, ask questions. Other workforce development professionals and colleagues, like accounting staff, are generally eager to share knowledge and experiences.

COMPETENCIES

- Understand the importance of market considerations and how they can influence resource allocation decisions.
- Identify the three key financial statements, the income statement, balance sheet, and statement of cash flows.
- Explain the purpose of the income statement, balance sheet, and statement of cash flows
- Distinguish monitoring activities from budget and planning activities
- Explain the purpose of the audit report and budget documents and how they differ
- Identify important non-financial measures that are related to finance and budgeting processes
- Understand the role of continuous improvement in workforce development

Part III

Special Issues Affecting Community College Workforce Development

Chapter Twelve

Factors Influencing the Retention and Persistence of African American and Latino Male STEM Students in Community College

Michael C. Wood

African American and Latino males who seek better opportunities and career development through their engagement in education must find ways to persist beyond their current educational environment to seize career opportunities that will improve their post-graduation prospects. Further, secondary and post-secondary institutions must continue to provide the types of opportunities that lead students down a path to long-term educational success. Education challenges, combined with socioeconomic challenges, are often a one-two knock-out punch for minorities, acting to severely curtail if not completely prevent prospects of long-term career development success.

Our goal is to explore the journey and experiences that inhibit underrepresented African American and Latino male community college students' from persisting to graduation and how we can improve their experiences relationship and academic pursuits on campus. Despite efforts to increase minority opportunities, prospects are still better for the White majority—to change this trend, minorities need greater support in navigating the broad array of social, political, economic, psychological, educational, and workforce development issues that are deeply rooted in the U.S. power structure.[1] Looking at education, and specifically at national levels of education achievement, the overall level of educational attainment in the United States is both low and stagnated regarding minority students.

FACTORS OF INFLUENCE

During the last several years I have had the pleasure of developing a Black and Latino Male Empowerment group at one of the local colleges in which I worked. This group was engaged in all facets of educational involvement both cognitively and non-cognitively. Persistence and retention among these two homogenous groups are closely monitored and expected outcomes were reviewed and revisited bi-weekly for efficacy and understanding.

Recently, my research led me to interview eight young men who were entering college and wanted to address their first or second year experiences. Our goal was to provide insight into their experience and provide solutions for their success. Our team noticed two prevailing themes, *Non-Cognitive Development* (see table 12.1) and *Deficit Thinking* as it relates to faculty, staff and peer groups, which greatly affected student outcomes along with their overall academic and cultural understanding of their environments.

Non-cognitive theory was initially introduced by sociologists Bowles and Gintis as an indicator of the overemphasis on cognitive skills regarding the determination of education and economic success. Non-cognitive skills could be classified in terms such as character skills, competencies, personality traits, life skills and soft skills, which also include additional characteristics such as motivation, confidence, tenacity, trustworthiness, perseverance, and social and communication skills.[2] Deficit Thinking refers to the notion that students (particularly low income, minority students) fail in school because such students and their families experience deficiencies that obstruct the learning process (e.g., limited intelligence, lack of motivation and inadequate home socialization).[3]

Valencia believed that the dominance of deficit thinking "blames the victim way of thinking" whereas failure among students is the result of "alleged internal deficiencies" (p. xi).[4] Although, deficit-thinking was reviewed we wanted to look at an *Anti-Deficit Thinking* mind set when it came to instructor, staff and peer-to-peer interaction with students of color on campus. Furthermore, Harrison suggested that "*Anti-deficit thinking* emerged as opposition to deficit thinking that contended ethnic minorities, and the poor, were the cause of their own socio-economic and educational attainment issues" (p. 12).[5]

Harper proposed an Anti-Deficit Achievement Framework for Minority Student Achievement (see figure 12.1) which may be employed to understand how various social agents can act to facilitate the achievement of racial/ethnic minority students.[6] An Anti-Deficit Achievement Framework could be applied at the institutional level to underscore the benefits of focusing on institutional factors that foster positive outcomes among African American and Latino males.

Table 12.1. Description of Non-Cognitive Variables

Variable Number	Variable Name	Description
1	Positive self-concept	Demonstrates confidence, strength of character, determination and independence
2	Realistic self-appraisal	Recognizes and accepts any strengths and deficiencies, especially academic, and works hard at self-development; recognizes need to broaden his or her individuality
3	Successfully handling the system (racism)	Exhibits a realistic view of the system on the basis of personal experience of racism; committed to improving the existing system; takes an assertive approach to dealing with existing wrongs, but is not hostile to society and is not a "cop-out"; able to handle racist system
4	Performance for long-term goals	Able to defer gratification; plans ahead and sets goals
5	Availability of strong support person	Seeks and takes advantage of a strong support network or has someone to turn to in crisis or for encouragement
6	Leadership experience	Demonstrates strong leadership in any area of his or her background (church), sports, non-educational groups, gang leaders and so on
7	Community involvement	Participates and is involved in his or her community
8	Knowledge acquired in the field	Acquires knowledge in a sustained or culturally related way in any field

EDUCATIONAL PERSISTENCE

Many of the socioeconomic barriers facing minority students begin with a lack of preparation or under-preparedness at the secondary level. Statistically, minorities lag behind their White counterparts beginning in elementary school, which then follows them through high school. These concerns are echoed in a growing academic literature on education. If no action is taken to remedy this disparity, large numbers of males will be left behind both socially and economically.

In other words, high school completion rates indicate direct economic impacts on the fiscal and financial future of each African American and

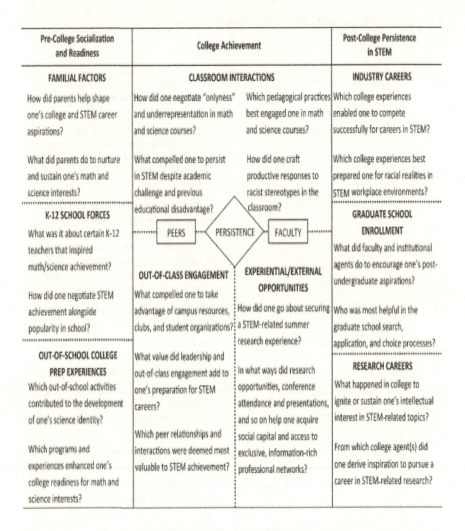

Figure 12.1. "Harper (2012), Black Male Student Success in Higher Education: A Report from the National Black Male College Achievement Study" (n.d.).

Latino male and their matriculation to community college. Both ethnicities are at high-risk of academic failure, dropout, suspension, expulsion, or referral to special education programs. Although educators and school administrators are often complicit in the marginalization of minorities, their actions alone are not altogether responsible for the social subordination of this group. Educators and policy makers must face the sobering fact that the U.S.'s economic future could rest upon the education of this emerging yet fragile workforce. Therefore, future studies must interrogate how education systems interface with other drivers of social, economic and workforce inequity.

THE ECONOMICS OF EDUCATION: FINANCIAL PERSISTENCE

For African American and Latino males, enrolling in community college means the completion of at least four critical tasks: (a) graduating from high school, (b) meeting minimal collegiate qualifications, (c) applying to the college or university of choice, and in many cases (d) finding the financial assistance needed to pay for their education.

The process of determining the cost of increasing African American and Latino males' ability to matriculate through college or university can be complicated, and have many factors, including socioeconomic status (SES), parental assistance and community college and university pricing, Escalating tuition costs and fees are increasing the number of community college students who depend on financial aid to gain access to higher education.

For many African American and Latino males, the federal government's Pell Grant program provides the financial assistance needed to attend and afford entry and admission to college. Their persistence and ultimate success in college stem from a multifaceted set of processes that start prior to their junior and senior years in high school. African American and Latino males could research several questions prior to his entry into the collegiate ranks:

1. What are the graduation rates of African American Latino males where prospective students will attend?
2. How do grant/loan programs affect student and parental decisions and behaviors during middle school and early high school years that may influence community college participation?
3. How do student grant/loan programs affect enrollment rates and decisions about where to attend?
4. How do grant/loan programs affect college persistence, performance, success, and completion?

HUMAN CAPITAL INVESTMENT

Educational neglect has affected the participation in and graduation rates of minority students in higher education. The United States political and educational infrastructure must view minorities as "Human Capital." Human capital represents productive capacities useful to employers, such as general educational development, labor force experience, and work habits.[7]

A community college education is a first step within collective processes and offers a potential cultural shift that educators, politicians, and private sector employers should embrace. Training within the community college infrastructure would allow our underrepresented population to leap forward economically.

Former President Barack Obama launched an "Educate to Innovate" campaign to improve the participation and performance of America's students in science, technology, engineering, and mathematics (STEM).[8] This campaign included efforts from the federal government and leading companies, foundations, non-profits, and science and engineering societies to help young people across America excel in science and math. This initiative is designed to increase literacy in areas of STEM, develop student awareness in STEM education, while expanding and extending STEM education and career advancement for underrepresented groups. Although, minorities are entering STEM fields, they are not persisting to graduation in the same numbers as their White and Asian counterparts. Solutions like these must promote educational opportunity, economic growth and stability for African American and Latino males within the community college system and facilitate their efforts to climb the corporate ladder. Additionally, minority students must actively seek and be in engaged in STEM opportunities that strengthen their economic footprint.

CHANGING THE WORKFORCE LANDSCAPE

According to the U.S. Department of Labor and Statistics unemployment rates for October 2017, seasonally adjusted/not seasonally adjusted, were 13.9 percent and 19.3 percent, respectively, for African American and Latino males aged 16 to 19. These economic indicators must be addressed.[9] What are some of the challenges and choices faced by minorities when it comes to career development? Historically, minorities have held positions that have been inferior to their abilities.

The white-dominated U.S. culture has often depicted minoritized population as intellectually inferior. While this indicator of white dominance has become less prominent, aspects remain in the sub-culture of the workplace. Minority educators and students still face unique problems in dealing with oppressive attitudes, policies, and culturally insensitive practices. Students of color must be the change agents concerning this perception; they must find an appropriate space within which to wrestle with the inherent dichotomy of learning and working in organizations designed according to a value system that, in most cases, stands in opposition to their cultural background.

PROGRAM MODELING

One significant program that can be analyzed for its success in producing and preparing African American and Latino male students for leadership in the STEM field is the Meyerhoff Scholars Program. Founded by Robert and Jane Meyerhoff with administrative assistance from Freeman Hrabowski, President at University of Maryland Baltimore County (UMBC) in 1988. The Meyerhoff Scholars Program leads in its effort to increase diversity among future leaders in science, technology, engineering, and math-related fields.

The Meyerhoff program has produced more than 1,400 scholars and over 1,100 alumni across the nation, with more than 300 students enrolled in graduate and professional programs. Meyerhoff's mission is to ensure that all students achieve given the proper guidance and support (UMBC 2019[10]). The Meyerhoff Scholars Program provides the following:

- Recruiting of minority students in math and science;
- A summer bridge program;
- Comprehensive merit scholarship support;
- Active faculty involvement in recruiting, teaching, and students' research experiences;
- Strong programmatic values including high achievement, study groups, tutoring, and preparing for graduate or professional school;
- Substantive research experiences for students;
- Intensive academic advising and personal counseling;
- Active involvement of the entire campus;
- Linking students with mentors;
- A strong sense of community among the students;
- Communication with the students' families; and
- Continuous evaluation and documentation of program outcomes.

Although Meyerhoff has a very selective screening process, the template that has been set for students in community college and STEM programming is very significant. Meyerhoff has had a dramatic impact on the number of minority students succeeding in STEM fields; students were 5.3 times more likely to have graduated from or to be currently attending a STEM PhD or MD/PhD program resulting from their involvement in Meyerhoff.

With the need to develop additional underrepresented students in STEM a new partnership developing between the University of Maryland, Baltimore County (UMBC), the Pennsylvania State University, the University of North Carolina at Chapel Hill (UNC), and the Howard Hughes Medical Institute (HHMI) has great promise. These four universities have launched a collaborative Meyerhoff Adaptation Project to study if elements of UMBC's highly regarded Meyerhoff Scholars Program can be adapted at Penn State and UNC.

The contributing schools intend to learn what it takes to establish a successful program, and then share what is learned so other institutions might follow. This initiative could provide a unique opportunity for community colleges to adapt Meyerhoff into their educational structures.[11] The supportive nature of this program and others like it will better prepare African American and Latino male students as they begin their community college careers.

LESSONS LEARNED: GROWTH INITIATIVES

Literature located thus far indicates a need for continued initiatives which ensure minorities gain the opportunities needed to have an educational and economic voice. Persistence is not just a minority student issue—it is a societal issue. The best way to improve economic opportunity and reduce inequality is to increase the educational attainment skills of the U.S. workforce. Inequity in both education and the workplace regarding relational issues is one of several societal challenges faced by a changing workforce. For these reasons, supplementary questions require additional research:

1. Is there a value or benefit to having community colleges work directly with high schools to promote persistence for minorities? *(collaborative learning is an essential element regarding student success. The exposure of the collegiate lifestyle for high school age students and the mentorship community college students can and should provide will greatly enhance outreach programming for each entity).*
2. What strategies and best practices can be used to increase minority participation in STEM? *(provide academic and social support; integrate meaningful preparation in K–12; review college affordability; helps as tuition continues to increase above the rate increases of inflation; provide access, inclusiveness, and motivation as key elements to underrepresented student's interaction in STEM).*
3. What educational initiatives should be modeled as a next step and/or best practice? *(student could be involved in campus organizations, academic groups, ROTC, athletics, campus resources and counseling centers and non-academic student support groups which are a needed respite from the day-to-day grind of their academic pursuits).*
4. How can educators close the achievement gap between minorities and their White and Asian counterparts? *(educators and institutions can assist in laying a foundation for cultural interaction, relationship development, and soft skill development).*

5. What roles should community colleges play regarding developing a greater understanding of the minority students' educational and economic needs? *(provide authentic peer-to-staff interaction and cultivate meaningful relationships, communication and provide a sense of care).*
6. What must minority students accomplish to better position themselves for a changing economy? *(continue to develop, critical observation, language skills, time management, teamwork and leadership skills, communication and problem-solving skills).*
7. How can continued educational and ethnic stereotypes be addressed both educationally and, in the workplace? *(by promoting inclusiveness and intentionally promoting cultural exposure through constant self-appraisal and ongoing evaluation).*

CONCLUSION

In 2009 President Obama asked every American to commit to at least one year or more of higher education or career training. This is where community colleges have a distinct advantage over four-year institutions with regard to course offerings. Across the country, employers are more frequently reporting a "high need" for training programs in applied skills rather than basic skills. Faced with these facts, it is clear, continued effort must be made to ensure that minority students persist through secondary, postsecondary, and career technical schools to prepare for the ever-changing workforce. These groups must no longer lag behind white counterparts both educationally and economically.

The U.S. must continue to develop workforce and STEM educational curricula that will allow all persons, including minority students, to compete well into the twenty-first century. At the 2012 U.S. News STEM Solutions Leadership Summit, Antonio Flores, CEO of the Hispanic Association of Colleges and Universities, postulated that nearly 75 percent of children born by 2030 will be people of color; by 2050 the majority of school-aged children will be Latino; and 74 percent of the labor force will be Latino in the coming years. This shift from minority to majority means that race, ethnicity, and culture will undoubtedly play a more important role in science, technology, engineering and math fields. Based upon U.S. demographic shifts, policymakers and educators at the local, state, and federal levels must work collectively and collaboratively to enhance workforce and educational experiences for all students so that they can continue to enhance their skill sets to stay competitive in the global marketplace and keep the U.S. economy on a competitive footing.

The social experience of students can take many trajectories, some constructive and others deleterious. The opportunity to network with peers and engage in socially constructive initiatives can have a profound effect on their ability to establish lifelong relationships. One common theme expressed by our students was a desire for greater interpersonal relationships with faculty and staff. Halawah postulated that "student-faculty informal interpersonal relationships were measured in six components: academic integration, peer relations, social integration, informal faculty relations, faculty concern, and student commitment" (670).[12]

The development of constructive relationships for African American and Latino males is an educational imperative. These informal relations can enhance or hinder students' personal and professional growth. The use of a Cultural Climate Survey (see textbox 12.1) could greatly assist career educators and leaders to better understand the social experience of each student on their campus. One of the successful methodologies considered for student achievement through mentorship could be the WISE method, where the mentor can view:

- *W - Whole person,* College students must be viewed as more than a GPA, a scholarship recipient, an athlete, or a deficit-oriented statistic.
- *Promote I - Intrusive accountability,* Successful programs understand the non-negotiable necessity to build in an accountability system.
- *Engage in S - Sustained,* systemic, support. No program or initiative, regardless of its level of importance or initial fanfare, is able to make a lasting impact into the lives of its participants without the sustained, sanctioned support of the organization's leadership and
- *E - Exposure to success,* insisting that students are exposed to an array of varied expressions of success is a component central to the best mentoring programs.[13]

TEXTBOX 12.1. CULTURAL ATTITUDES AND CLIMATE SURVEY

This questionnaire examines attitudes and beliefs about issues important to racial and ethnic diversity at your institution. Your honest responses are very important in studying these issues on the campus. All responses are anonymous. Thank you for your participation.

GENERAL INSTRUCTIONS: Read each item carefully and circle or check your response.

Racial and Ethnic Climate

1. Please indicate how much you agree with the following statements: Strongly Disagree – 1; Disagree – 2; Neutral – 3; Agree – 4; Strongly Agree – 5; Not Applicable – NA

    a. My experiences since coming to school here have led me to become more understanding of racial/ethnic differences. 1 2 3 4 5 NA
    b. Getting to know people with racial/ethnic backgrounds different from my own has been easy on this campus. 1 2 3 4 5 NA
    c. My social interactions on this campus are largely confined to students of my race/ethnicity. 1 2 3 4 5 NA
    d. I feel there are expectations about my academic performance because of my race/ethnicity. 1 2 3 4 5 NA
    e. I feel pressured to participate in ethnic activities at this school. 1 2 3 4 5 NA
    f. I feel I need to minimize various characteristics of my racial/ethnic culture (e.g. language, dress) to be able to fit in here. 1 2 3 4 5 NA
    g. My experiences since coming to this school have strengthened my own sense of ethnic identity. 1 2 3 4 5 NA

2. Think about the faculty whose courses you have taken here. How many of them would you describe as: None – 1; Few – 2; Some – 3; Most – 4; All – 5; Not Applicable – NA

    a. Approachable outside of the classroom? 1 2 3 4 5 NA
    b. Fair to all students regardless of their racial or ethnic backgrounds? 1 2 3 4 5 NA

3. Think about your experiences in the classroom. Please indicate how much you agree with the following statements: Strongly Disagree – 1; Disagree – 2; Neutral – 3; Agree – 4; Strongly Agree – 5; Not Applicable – NA

    a. In my experience, students of different racial/ethnic backgrounds participate equally in classroom discussion and learning. 1 2 3 4 5 NA
    b. I feel I am expected to represent my race or ethnic group in discussions in class. 1 2 3 4 5 NA

c. Faculty use examples relevant to people of my race/ethnic group in their lectures. 1 2 3 4 5 NA
d. In my classes I feel that my professors ignore my comments or questions. 1 2 3 4 5 NA

4. Please indicate how comfortable you feel in the following situations at this school: Very Uncomfortable – 1; Uncomfortable – 2; Neutral – 3; Comfortable – 4; Very Comfortable – 5; Not Applicable – NA

   a. Going to see a faculty member of my own race/ethnicity. 1 2 3 4 5 NA
   b. Speaking with others about my racial/ethnic background. 1 2 3 4 5 NA
   c. Being in situations where I am the only person of my racial/ethnic group. 1 2 3 4 5 NA
   d. Saying what I think about racial/ethnic issues. 1 2 3 4 5 NA
   e. Being with people whose racial/ethnic backgrounds are different from my own. 1 2 3 4 5 NA
   f. Participating in class. 1 2 3 4 5 NA
   g. Going to see a faculty member of a different race/ethnicity than my own. 1 2 3 4 5 NA
   h. Being with people whose racial/ethnic backgrounds are the same as my own. 1 2 3 4 5 NA

How Well is This School Doing on Diversity?

1. The effort made by your school to improve relations and understanding between people of different racial/ethnic background is: Too little; About right; Too much; Don't know
2. Please indicate to what degree you agree with the following statements: Strongly Disagree – 1; Disagree – 2; Neutral – 3; Agree – 4; Strongly Agree – 5; Not Applicable – NA

   a. The campus has done a good job providing programs and activities that promote multicultural understanding. 1 2 3 4 5 NA
   b. At this school students are resentful of others whose race/ethnicity is different from their own. 1 2 3 4 5 NA
   c. There should have a requirement for graduation that students take at least one course on the role of ethnicity and race in society. 1 2 3 4 5 NA

  d. This school does not promote respect for diversity. 1 2 3 4 5 NA
  e. The student newspaper's coverage of racial/ethnic events and issues is balanced. 1 2 3 4 5 NA
  f. Diversity is was one of the reasons why I chose to come here. 1 2 3 4 5 NA

3. Which racial/ethnic groups should the school make special efforts to recruit as students and as faculty? (please check all that apply)

  a. Hispanic Americans
  b. Native Americans
  c. Asian Americans
  d. African Americans
  e. None – no special efforts should be taken to recruit any particular racial/ethnic group members

General Experience on Campus

1. Please indicate to what degree you agree with the following statements: Strongly Disagree – 1; Disagree – 2; Neutral – 3; Agree – 4; Strongly Agree – 5; Not Applicable – NA

  a. The school provides an environment for the free and open expression of ideas opinions and beliefs. 1 2 3 4 5 NA
  b. Overall my educational experience here has been a rewarding one. 1 2 3 4 5 NA
  c. The atmosphere in my classes does not make me feel like I belong. 1 2 3 4 5 NA
  d. I would recommend this school to siblings or friends as a good place to go to college. 1 2 3 4 5 NA
  e. The overall quality of academic programs here is excellent. 1 2 3 4 5 NA
  f. I feel as though I belong in the campus community. 1 2 3 4 5 NA

Your Experiences on Campus

1. Please use the scale below to indicate the extent to which you believe each of the following is present at your school: Little or None – 1; Some – 2; Quite A Bit – 3; A Great Deal – 4; Not Applicable – NA

    a. racial conflict on campus. 1 2 3 4 NA
    b. respect by faculty for students of different racial and ethnic groups. 1 2 3 4 NA
    c. respect by students for other students of different racial and ethnic groups. 1 2 3 4 NA
    d. racial/ethnic separation on campus. 1 2 3 4 NA
    e. school commitment to the success of students of different racial and ethnic groups. 1 2 3 4 NA
    f. friendship between students of different racial and ethnic groups. 1 2 3 4 NA
    g. interracial tensions in the residence halls. 1 2 3 4 NA
    h. interracial tensions in the classroom. 1 2 3 4 NA

2. How fairly do you believe you have been treated by the following: Very Unfairly – 1; Unfairly – 2; Neutral – 3; Fairly – 4; Very Fairly – 5; No Interaction – NA

    a. university police. 1 2 3 4 5 NA
    b. residence hall personnel. 1 2 3 4 5 NA
    c. faculty. 1 2 3 4 5 NA
    d. teaching assistants. 1 2 3 4 5 NA
    e. students. 1 2 3 4 5 NA

3. In each of these settings to what extent have you been exposed to information about the history culture and/or social issues of racial and ethnic groups other than whites? Not At All – 1; A Little – 2; Some – 3; Quite A Bit – 4; A Great Deal – 5; Not Applicable – NA

    a. in course readings lectures and discussions. 1 2 3 4 5 NA
    b. in activities and programs in the residence halls. 1 2 3 4 5 NA
    c. in other school programs or activities. 1 2 3 4 5 NA
    d. in informal interactions and conversations with friends. 1 2 3 4 5 NA

4. How many for-credit courses have you taken from faculty members of the following racial/ethnic groups on this campus?

   a. Hispanic Americans
   b. Native Americans
   c. Asian Americans
   d. African Americans
   e. Not sure of race/ethnicity of faculty member

5. How many courses have you taken here that have focused primarily on the culture history or social concerns of:

   a. racial and ethnic groups (other than whites) in the U.S.?

   Number of Courses:

   b. non-Western racial and ethnic groups outside the U.S.?

   Number of Courses:

6. How often do you have difficulty getting help or support from: Never – 1; Seldom – 2; Sometimes – 3; Often – 4; Not Applicable – NA

   a. faculty. 1 2 3 4 NA
   b. students. 1 2 3 4 NA
   c. teaching assistants. 1 2 3 4 NA

7. How often have you been exposed to a racist atmosphere created by the faculty? Never – 1; Seldom – 2; Sometimes – 3; Often – 4; Not Applicable – NA

   a. in the classroom. 1 2 3 4 NA
   b. outside the classroom. 1 2 3 4 NA

8. How often have you been exposed to a racist atmosphere created by other students? Never – 1; Seldom – 2; Sometimes – 3; Often – 4; Not Applicable – NA

   a. in the classroom. 1 2 3 4 NA
   b. outside the classroom. 1 2 3 4 NA

9. Please indicate whether your experience here has changed your behavior in any of the following ways: YES OR NO

   a. I now recognize culturally-biased behavior I had not previously identified. YES NO
   b. I now discuss topics related to cultural awareness with friends. YES NO
   c. I now stop myself from using language that may be offensive to others. YES NO
   d. I now handle negative language used by another in such a way as to try to educate the other person. YES NO
   e. I now initiate contact with people who are not of my culture or ethnic background. YES NO

Diversity Programs

1. Have you attended or participated in any diversity programs on campus this year?

   Yes
   No
   Don't Know

2. To what degree do you agree that attending programs on diversity contributes to the goal of building community?

   Strongly Disagree
   Disagree
   Neutral
   Agree
   Strongly Agree
   Not Applicable

Your Intentions for the Future

1. Do you plan to return to school here next semester?

   Yes
   No
   Don't Know

2. If you do not return to school here do you think you will transfer to another college or university?

   Yes

No
Don't Know

3. Please indicate your current major:
4. Please indicate your cumulative GPA:

   3.5 - 4.0
   3.0 - 3.4
   2.5 - 2.99
   2.0 - 3.49
   below 2.0

5. Please indicate your current place of residence *(check one only)*:

   Residence hall?
   Fraternity or Sorority house?
   Off-campus rental housing/apartment?
   Home of parents or relatives?
   Own home?
   Other (please specify)?

Please tell us what you think the school could do differently to improve campus climate with regard to diversity.

Thank you very much for completing this survey. Your efforts will help the school in its efforts to provide a quality education to students.

The tradeoff in balancing friendships, extracurricular activities and organizing one's daily routine collegiately is an adjustment that each student must learn how to manage. Time management and the academic demands placed upon students will quickly open their eyes to the reality of the day-to-day rigors of pursuing a degree and workforce readiness opportunities. A student's ability to master this concept will further enhance his or her ability to grow academically!

The development of relationships in college can be the beginning of a lifelong commitment to stay engaged with one's peers. The social capital invested and the supportive nature of a person's affiliation with peers can be insightful, invigorating, thought-provoking and motivating. Davis believed that the "social bonds and supportive interactions are important to a person's health and well-being" (143).[14] Researchers have found that support networks, which include family, peers, and mentors, help facilitate adjustment to college.

NOTES

1. Bowen, W G., M. M. Chingos, and M. S. McPherson. *Crossing the Finish Line: Completing College at America's Public Universities*. Princeton, NJ: Princeton University Press, 2009.
2. Bowles, S. and H Gintis. *Schooling in Capitalist America* (Vol. 75). New York: n.p., 1976.
3. Valencia, R. R. *Dismantling Contemporary Deficit Thinking: Educational Thought and Practice* (Critical Educator). Routledge: New York, NY, 2010.
4. Valencia, *Dismantling Contemporary Deficit Thinking*.
5. Harrison, M. C. *A Narrative Inquiry of Successful Black Male College Students*. n.p.: n.p., 2014.
6. Harper, S. R. "Leading the Way: Inside the Experiences of High-Achieving African American Male Students." n.p.: About Campus, 10(1), 8–15, 2005.
7. Lutz, W. "Global Human Capital: Integrating Education and Population." *Science*, 333(6042), 587–92. New York, NY. doi: n.p., 2011.
8. "Educate to Innovate." Campaign for Excellence in Science, Technology, Engineering & Math (Stem) Education. n.p.: n.p., n.d..
9. Department of Labor and Statistics (October 2017). n.p.: Retrieved From https://www.bls.gov/news.release/archives/empsit_11032017.pdf, n.d..
10. Retrieved from. n.p.: n.p., n.d..
11. Retrieved September 5, 2019.
12. Halawah, I. "The Impact of Student-Faculty Informal Interpersonal Relationships on Intellectual and Personal Development." n.p.: *College Student Journal, 40*(3), 670, 2006.
13. Kelly, H. D. and P. M. Christian. "(2014, January)." (n.d.):
14. Davis, R. B. "Social Support Networks and Undergraduate Student Academic-Success-Related Outcomes: A Comparison of Black Students on Black and White Campuses." In *College in Black and White: African American Students in Predominantly White and in Historically Black Public Universities*, edited by W. R. Allen, E. G. Epps, and N. Z. Haniff, 143–57. New York: State University of New York Press, 1991.

Chapter Thirteen

Dealing with the Changing Face of Workforce Development

Victor Rodgers

In our current employment dynamic, we face many different challenges; a "Silver Tsunami" of retiring Baby Boomers, smaller households producing fewer potential workers, and demographic shifts being just a few. These and other factors have produced a renewed focus on workforce development. There is not a Chamber meeting, industry summit, or economic development discussion where 'workforce development' is not mentioned prominently, with the ongoing concern on how this issue is affecting the economic prosperity of our community's. The numbers of unfilled jobs, and the shortage of potential workers is dire indeed.

A fair question which should/could be asked is "what exactly is workforce development?" A lack of a skilled workforce to replace our aging personnel infrastructure is a workforce problem. The dearth of qualified health care professionals to deal with our aging population is another workforce problem. The introduction of AI and automation is another workforce problem; problem being defined as influencing the workplace dynamics involving people.

Workforce development on the other hand is, to quote Dr. Sygielski, the president of Harrisburg Area Community College in Harrisburg, Pennsylvania, "creative problem solving." The best workforce development entities are those that look at, and clearly identify, the problem. They then develop specific "fixes" to the identified issue. Unfortunately, too many workforce development entities develop "fixes" for problems without really getting to the root cause.

Often this comes from acting on assumptions and stereotypes of situations or people, which is perfectly normal; we all develop "shortcuts." A recent example of this type of tunnel vision was present in a recent meeting which focused on ways we could mitigate the poverty situation within our community with various workforce practitioners. This group met to discuss ways to address poverty in the inner city by providing workforce training to a community with lots of challenges.

The group of workforce development professionals, community leaders, and business partners discussed several factors deemed important to the situation; we talked about childcare being a detriment, the lack of transportation, and of course the lack of skills. The group went back and forth in the discussion; lack of passion was not a problem of this group. While there were many great ideas put forth to deal with some of these challenges, the one factor that failed to make it into the discussion was the difference in culture. This is not a difference between ethnic backgrounds, but a difference between the cultures of someone battling poverty every day, and what the cultural expectations and differences are for an employee. Since this was never discussed, the creative solution was never designed.

In most workforce development discussions this is a typical outcome; we come up with some great strategies to mitigate those other factors (transportation, childcare, etc.), without addressing the culture shock unemployed and underemployed people face when they are thrust into the cultural expectations from the world of work. Again this requires creative problem solving. With this unresolved barrier, it's no wonder so many programs fail. We spend very little time addressing the real underlying cause, often cultural competencies, while spending millions on training programs.

We must do better because we simply have no other choice. We are going to have to engage with every available sector of our community because we are losing skilled workers at a rate that is truly alarming. Why is this new focus on cultural competencies necessary? What's changed so drastically that this needs to be a focused effort for our workforce communities across the country? Let me tell you a quick story on fishing.

Think about our various industrial and business sectors as fishermen, and the fish they go after as new employees. For years, in some cases decades, they have been successful fishing in the same location. Since they've been fishing at that same hole, they know where to stand, what time to fish, what bait to use, and what rod and reel they'd need to be successful. The fish they were looking for were typically white males, but the occasional person of color or woman was also caught. Many of our workforce delivery systems and programs were set up to support this style of fishing.

Now, to put it bluntly, that fishing hole has almost dried up, and we're going to have to fish in areas that we've not traditionally considered. To name a few: Reentrants, chronically unemployed, non-native English speakers, people of color and women as well as earlier engagement with high schoolers. This means when we investigate those different areas to fish, we'll also need to use different bait, fish at different times, etc. In reality, our entire approach will need to be different.

This means workforce development professionals must be intentional when we speak about workforce development and look at creating solutions that work. We will need to engage with people/organizations who know these communities and who can help us design programs which are specific to the various cultures we hope to target. This means designing programs which specifically allow us to catch a different kind of "fish," while understanding the culture they come from. To do that we'll need to develop partnerships which allows for the sharing of resources.

PARTNERSHIPS

Over the years there have been a continuing series of meetings to discuss the workforce challenges which have been building year by year. The workforce development systems and the employers knew the "baby boomer" tide was coming, but we all looked at each other to solve the disruption it would inevitably bring. Business leaders pointed the finger at schools and demanded they produce kids who were ready for the workforce. Schools complained that they needed more direction from the business community (getting kids "work ready" is a little vague), and workforce development leadership for the most part kept humming along.

Out of necessity, that must change. The good news is that everyone now realizes that this is a problem that must be addressed collaboratively across the entire community. Business must be willing to put some "skin" into the game, and for the most they are. Schools (K–12) must realize that not only should they not plan for everyone to go to college, but they need to be intentional about Career and Technical Education as an option for all.

One area of opportunity for our systems would be to look at more allocation towards "projects." In accordance with the regulations which govern how resources are spent, Workforce Development Boards have to be focused on people with barriers, this is probably due to the assumption being that resources exist and are available for those without barriers, they just need to be accessed. What a tremendous opportunity relocating some of our funding could be if we could find creative ways to create those specialized projects which would be targeted toward those who need training, but would otherwise not be eligible. This would help because a lot of the training which could immediately impact business and industry as well as the individual, there is no easy access for those without barriers. In the community college world, the Pell Grants available for degree programs are not available to most workforce programs, so unless individuals can somehow find a way to pay out of pocket, they cannot access the training needed to change their lives.

By only focusing on the hardest to serve, those who would benefit from a slight lift cannot receive access to training unless they can afford it themselves. Think about the single mom or the graduate with only a high school diploma who is making a living in jobs paying low wages. They desperately need training but often lack the requisite skills which would allow them into the programs.

This is not a position that is advocating not assisting the hard to serve, but we need to be honest and acknowledge that in many cases, they require a huge amount of case management and support. Many of the barriers and challenges they face are long-term, and require a serious investment of time and resources, which our current system is designed to provide. While this is a worthwhile investment, we just need to be aware that in many cases we're talking years of support and resources. This is time that business and industry no longer have.

This is the crux of the problem; business and industry are not in the business of social work; they are looking for a partnership which can help them solve their workforce challenges. While we attempt to partner with them, we often give them potential employees which they cannot use despite how desperate they are for staffing.

How can we, the workforce development leadership, change this dynamic? If we could focus on those with less challenging barriers, the WDB's could make partnerships that provide the "win-win" scenario which we all aspire to. Far too many times, the program operators within the workforce system partner with businesses with the intent of finding a landing space for their clients instead of truly looking at the talent level the business required. If the barriers were removed, think about how many after-school trainings could happen in partnership with school districts.

There is money in the Workforce Investment and Opportunities Act (WIOA) for different groups which need training and assistance to find employment. There are training dollars for Adults, Dislocated Workers, and Youth programs. Examining the youth programs training is a prime example of the challenge our entrenched programs have. They are focused on the participant without understanding the needs of the employers. Our Youth program has two components: In-School, which deals with those in the K–12 system, and Out of School Youth, young men and women between the age of 18–24, who are out of high school, but need employment. Most Youth dollars are designed to be used on the Out of School Youth programs.

Again, this is a noble cause, but an extremely heavy lift. In fact, this is the most difficult demographic group to serve since many of them come with serious barriers to employment (educational deficits, some with criminal records, some already parenting). Having worked in a One-Stop shop for six years in the state of North Carolina, I found the most difficult program to manage was the Out of School Youth program. Due to the large number of barriers which many of them have, the program was often more of a social worker environment than a job readiness and placement program.

How can we realistically expect a true partnership with business and industry when we are not consistently providing them the quality workforce they need? This "disconnect" has many of the employers concerned with how the workforce systems in their region can help them overcome the workforce challenges they face; how can we work to increase the quality of workers presented to them as potential employees?

How could we better address this? Wouldn't it better suit the students and employers if some of those same resources could be repurposed towards In-School youth, and be used to create in-demand training? You could be creative on what the areas needs are, and direct students into training pathways into great employment opportunities. Just like some of our other communities, the K–12 system has not been targeted enough.

The key to any partnership is ensuring it's a "win-win" for all involved. In many cases, workforce development entities are seeking to reach out to business and industry with an eye towards making sure their program goals are met. Whether its job placement, or spending out end-of-year funds, rarely are we out to simply see what the real needs are. While business initially reaches out to us, unfortunately, in many cases, we're not hitting the mark. We continue to supply them with under qualified workers with the expectation that they'll train them. We forget that the businesses are into providing a product or service; they're not trainers!

Let me give you an example of a "win-win" partnership. We partnered with several school districts to provide training to their seniors who didn't have a plan after graduation. The model we used is a 140-hour training which focused on time management, conflict resolution, communication, and working in teams. They also received OSHA 10 and CPR/First Aide training. We called this the STEP Academy (Stand up, Take action, Expect results, Put in the work), and we partnered with local manufacturers so the students could have an opportunity to meet them, tour, and look at that potential career path. The STEP Academy will be discussed in greater detail later.

More importantly than the employment opportunities this led to, it also focused the attention of the manufacturers and schools on the lack of awareness early high schoolers were getting as it related to the manufacturing field. This led to them banding together and providing funding and equipment to transform one of our underutilized buildings into a manufacturing "lab" where area schools can send those students to develop an understanding of the manufacturing field.

In another instance of a "win-win" situation, a team of workforce program operators worked with a large retailer years ago in North Carolina. The retailer came into various communities, and completely disrupted the "main street" concept by offering the cheapest goods in the area. Not only did this lead to smaller stores closing, but a bunch of unemployed retail workers that they were quick to snap up. The company's business model at the time, was a little over minimum wage, with no other compensation.

At the time, we had a shortage of skilled workers in the area, specifically Pharmacy Technicians. This team approached the management of this store with a "win-win" conversation. Could they use the opportunity to offer training (paid for by Workforce Investment Act dollars, the program replaced by WIOA) to their best workers to provide an incentive? Due to their low wages, even though their workers were employed, they qualified for WIA Adult funding.

Their issue wasn't getting workers; they had a long line of people who were low skilled and wanted an opportunity to work in their retail environment. Their issue was that they had no way to incentivize and reward their best workers. This was a classic "win-win", since absolutely everyone benefitted. The workers who worked hard were given an opportunity for additional training. The store had a way to offer an incentive to get workers motivated to work harder, and we were able to address the Pharmacy tech shortage.

Workforce Development Boards should be asking their program operators to demonstrate those types of partnerships. All too often, they "partner" with a business entity, and while it appears the sole beneficiary is the business owner who gets workers (via the On the Job Training program), who are unskilled, but whose wages are offset by WIOA dollars, that's not really the case. Let's examine if this is a true partnership. The businesses are getting an unskilled worker who will cost them time and money to upskill despite the OJT funds. The worker is often not trained by the employer because they are used in an unskilled capacity. This ensures that if the economic conditions change for the worst, they are the "first fired." The only one who really benefits is the program operator who can count this as an employed participant if they stay employed past the reporting periods.

This is something that WDB's should examine as it relates to their program operators; in a time of almost full employment, when there's a "Hiring Now" sign on almost every business, is your program operator really maximizing the opportunity to assist your community by giving the employers money to hire someone?

Instead, wouldn't it make more sense to require innovative programming which creates skilled workers that are in demand? Heck, the employers would pay you if you provided them the talent they're looking for! Why don't more Boards and program operators operate under that umbrella? Unfortunately, it appears as if many in our workforce delivery systems across the country see their participants through the lens of the challenges they present instead of the potential that's there. That's perfectly normal, after all, the WIOA program guidelines are designed to assist the hardest to serve, as indicated by the eligibility requirements. However, to fully maximize the potential in our underserved and under-represented, we're going to have to get in the business of recognizing and nurturing talent.

This brings us to our next topic for conversation; how do you recognize talent? It's certainly not just by diplomas, certificates or other methods, including resumes. All those reflect that a person has spent the requisite amount of time necessary for completion; it doesn't say whether they are truly talented. The same can be said for a resume; it's a person's subjective evaluation of their work history and accomplishments. Subjective reflections rarely are an accurate measure of a person's talent. How then does a workforce professional and the community and businesses they serve fairly and accurately measure an individual's skill level; the answer is Work Keys.

WORK KEYS

Work Keys is a program created over thirty years ago by ACT, the college testing group. The genesis for the program was ACT's attempt to determine a workers eligibility for a specific occupation; like the college testing used to determine whether someone would be successful in a college environment.

The Work Keys credential, called the National Career Readiness Certificate (NCRC), has four categories: Bronze, Silver, Gold, and Platinum. All 22,000-plus occupations, which have been measured, fall somewhere in these four categories. Using this tool, it's an easy match to see a NCRC holder, and match that person to a position.

Hundreds of companies have used this to increase retention (they hire the right fit the first time), decrease training time and costs (the people being trained have the foundational skills to understand the information which speeds everything up). That last bit might need a little bit more of an explanation; have you ever been in training where the whole class was extended because the instructor had to teach to the slowest person in the training? Happens all the time, which increases the cost and time needed to train.

A perfect example would be a large, nationally known business in Pennsylvania which has fully adopted the Work Keys system. They hire based on foundational skills as identified through the individuals Work Keys credential. They also utilize succession planning which promotes from within using the same parameters of matching foundational skills to an opening within the company. This has the dual benefit of adding an objective factor to promotions, while also letting the workforce know what they need to have for consideration!

So how does this work? An individual's foundational skills are measured using the Work Keys assessment, and if they have the right level, they are hired into the corresponding occupation. It's that simple; if an occupation being advertised is rated as a "silver," then only someone with a Silver or above credential should apply or be hired for the job. We've all heard the stories of a good worker, who's promoted to a different position, and who's fired shortly after. They didn't stop being a good worker, they were promoted without assessing whether they had the foundational skills to do the new job they were being promoted into.

This is a situation which presents a perfect opportunity for a workforce development professional to lead. Businesses are in the business of producing either a product or service. They are not in the business of designing workforce development solutions. That is where we can add a level of expertise which they lack.

This is a program designed for business; let me repeat; this is a program designed for business! It is important to reiterate this because too many workforce development practitioners across the country often put the cart before the horse, meaning they eagerly use the program for their participants without partnering with business first. This completely invalidates the program, because if business doesn't recognize/value the program, it's useless to the participant. Let's discuss how we can use this product for the participant.

In workforce development conferences and events throughout the country, the statement is often voiced about the "skills gap." It's normally in the content of the growing shortage of skilled workers across all occupations. A reasonable response should be that there is a difference between having a trained worker and having a conversation about a skills gap. A trained worker is someone who has the certificate/credential in a profession. They've achieved this through formal training or by working in the profession. A Skills gap is when you believe there are not enough incumbent workers or new hires who possess the skills a business need.

The question we must ask is "how do you know you have a skills gap when you don't know the skill level of your current employees or the skill levels of those seeking employment with your company"? Just because someone has the credential/certificate doesn't mean they necessarily have the "skill" to do the job. To be clear, this does not include industry credentials such as NIMS, MSSC, etc. So, unless you have a way to measure the skills people have, you don't know if you have a true skills gap or not. A certificate/credential means they attended and passed a set of instructions/tests; so, they have the training. It doesn't mean they have the skill.

That is what the Work Keys program does, it measures an individual's skill set, and matches it against an occupation that's been analyzed as we previously discussed. An employer can have their jobs measured against a jobs data base, and then have their employees tested to see if they are "in the right seat." Basically, do they have the right "foundational skills" for the job they're in? This also allows employers to identify hidden talent and the ability to ensure they are investing scarce training dollars on the right people.

Imagine the value a workforce development entity could bring to the discussion if they were able to use Work Keys to solve the "skills gap" problem? Now many states are utilizing this amazing product, but it only works when business realizes the value. So, let's look at the typical one-stop. While we talk about helping the entire spectrum of job seekers, unless it's a dislocated worker rapid response, we're typically dealing with the hardest to serve. We work on resumes, in some cases support training for our participants, and try to get people a chance at an employment situation.

With all that, we're still dealing with the hard to serve and the barriers they bring (remember they must have barriers to qualify for the training dollars). Instead of trying to shiny them up for potential employers, what if we were very intentional about working with our business community, chambers, and economic developers to make sure the value of the NCRC was known, understood, and that Work Keys was adopted through those communities?

As we increasingly work with non-traditional members of the community, we need to show the value that they bring. Unfortunately, as mentioned earlier, we're too busy looking at the challenges these groups bring instead of the opportunity they represent. Again, let's imagine we are providing the creative solution versus retreading the same old programs.

Our team recently partnered with a Community Organization which traditionally deals with an inner-city, largely Black and Latino community struggling with poverty. We used Work Keys as an assessment tool to identify their skills level, and then partnered with a local Health Care Organization who paid for their training as Medical Assistants. Again, creative solutions, partnerships, and assessment.

Another program we gave to the participants was a STEP class, which was previously mentioned when talking about our High School partnerships. Remember the conversation earlier about acknowledging cultural differences? We must not only recognize the cultural differences; we must actively train them so that they know what the cultural expectations of the workplace are; that's where STEP comes in.

STEP (STAND UP, TAKE ACTION, EXPECT RESULTS, AND PUT IN THE WORK)

The genesis of the STEP program was due to our interaction with our business community. They were consistent in their assessment that the workers answering their ads didn't possess the soft skills necessary to be part of their teams; soft skills being defined as communication skills, being able to work effectively in teams, appropriate conflict resolution, and time management to name a few. This goes back to the cultural competencies mentioned earlier in the chapter; there is a "work culture" that has its own unspoken rules, expected conduct, etc., if you're not familiar with that culture, it can be a difficult transition.

Imagine you're a reentrant, trying to transition back into the outside world. You're leaving the culture of the institution, which has guided your every waking moment, and reentering society. One of the first things you are directed to do is to find employment (many of the Reentrants must pay victim restitution, court costs, child support, etc.). In many cases you don't have a skill and are expected to bring in the type of money necessary to pay those court ordered costs.

On top of these challenges, even if you can find gainful employment, you've got to adjust to a new culture! It's no wonder the recidivism rate is so high: the deck is stacked against them from the beginning. These two events—the lack of soft skills, and the problems our Reentrants faced—were what sparked the creation of the STEP Academy. The Community College had always worked with Reentrants—just not in a very effective way. Giving someone skills is important, but helping them understand and navigate through the cultural competencies of the workplace was even more important. I don't care how skilled you are; if you don't fit into the team, you're not keeping that job.

We started the STEP Academy with that premise in mind. A local non-profit provided professional dress, and we started every day with a handshake and a greeting. Knowing the students couldn't get back to their halfway houses for lunch, we created an additional partnership with another nonprofit which provided food so they could have a meal during the day.

We then started working on all of the "soft skills" mentioned above. Every day was role playing, video's, walking them through situations they were sure to find themselves in at some point of their work life, and giving them advice on how they could select the best decision. This was important, because when you do not have a lot of resources, when things happen you're liable to be stuck. A perfect example is transportation. When you've put all your resources into getting a car so that you can make it to work, what do you do when the car breaks down? Just not going to work is not an option because you need to keep the job. Training people to look for alternatives before they need them is the key.

When you hear about programs which offer "work readiness" classes, usually they consist of giving someone a resume and mock interviews. Think about your work readiness programs: do they really consist of soft skills training or is your team more focused on giving them a portfolio for a job search? If it's only a slight touch, you might not be giving the participant exactly what they need to be successful. Our STEP Academy is four weeks long, with the addition of computer basics, and utilizing the remedial software of Work Keys to work on their foundational skill.

How successful was the program? Let's look at the following stats:

1. We served 107 reentrants overall.
2. Of those 107, 79 graduated (there were a variety of reasons participants didn't complete; some left the area, some found employment, some were dismissed for not following attendance/behavior rules.
3. Of those 79 graduates, 55 decided to attend additional skilled training in either CNC Machining, Welding, or Office Professional.
4. Of those 55, all were still employed one year after completion.

Great numbers, especially with this population, but we didn't do it by ourselves. We created the partnerships mentioned above. We also partnered with business and industry in a couple of ways. They came in to handle our "mock" interviews so the participants were put in realistic hiring situations, and they created landing spots within their organizations.

We also partnered with civic and elected leaders, who attended and spoke at the graduations and really welcomed the participants back into the community. One of the largest factors was the attitudes and cooperation of the participants. We had a very strict absenteeism policy as well as a dress code and they met and exceeded our expectations. When I mentioned seeing the potential instead of the challenges, this was a perfect example.

As you can tell, the STEP Academy has morphed into serving all parts of the community. From the hardest to serve, to high schoolers, we customize and change it to fit the demographics we're dealing with; this year we'll have our first STEP Academy for our Latino population. Using a mix of English as a Second Language (ESL) curriculum, and the STEP curriculum, we hope to serve that community and help them transition into better opportunities.

CONCLUSION

Hopefully this has given you a few ideas on how you, as a workforce development professional, can bring immediate value to your various communities. Whether they be business and industry, communities of color, reentrants, unemployed or underemployed, there are tremendous opportunities to collaboratively solve the workforce challenges we have across the country. The key is creating partnerships that are developed to produce a "win-win." I spoke about the Work Keys program because I believe it to be the best tool to assess talent and skill. Lastly, we must understand that different segments of our community have different cultural norms which need to be addressed. You need to partner with those communities so that you understand where they're coming from. This will also dictate your programming to give them the awareness of the workplace culture they'll need if they are to be successful in the workplace.

Lastly, please keep this thought in mind: if you want to have successful programs with whatever group you're working with, see your participants as people with potential, not people with barriers. Good luck!

Chapter Fourteen

Conceptualizing Future Competencies Needed by Community College Workforce Development Practitioners

William J. Rothwell, Patrick E. Gerity, and Vernon L. Carraway

For many years experts have debated which comes first—organizational strategy or the organizational structure (organizational, job, and task design) needed to support strategy execution. While strategy ultimately "won" that contest, practitioners more recently question—in an age when innovation trumps information technology, manufacturing or agriculture as a source of competitive advantage—whether talent precedes strategy. After all, no organization would exist without a talented person or group that came up with the ideas that created that organization. Microsoft would not exist without Bill Gates; Apple would not exist in its current form without Steve Jobs; Walmart would not exist in its current form without Sam Walton; and, IBM would not exist as it does today without Tom Watson.

The same principle applies to Community College Workforce Development. While Community College leaders establish the purpose and mission of the workforce development effort, the people who create and implement the strategy for workforce development are critically important for successful strategy execution. And it does not require much of a stretch of the imagination to suggest that, in the future, the skills needed by workforce development practitioners in community colleges will change as economic conditions change, technological conditions change, work and working conditions change, and the role of community college workforce development professionals change.

But exactly what are competencies? How are they traditionally identified and used? What trends are shaping the future? How can the future competencies needed by workforce development practitioners be identified? And how can they be used? This chapter addresses these important questions and thereby points the way toward a next generation of community college workforce development professionals.

WHAT ARE COMPETENCIES?

There is no standard definition of the word "competency." But one fact seems clear: job descriptions summarize the work; competencies describe the human beings who perform that work. A job description is thus a work description; a competency model is a worker description. While different definitions of competencies stem from different ways of thinking about what matters in human productivity, it seems clear that if decision-makers clarify, in measurable terms, what results they want from any job, it is possible to work backward to list the characteristics of a person who can achieve those results.

HOW ARE COMPETENCIES TRADITIONALLY IDENTIFIED AND USED?

Traditionally, competencies are identified in one of three ways.

The first way is to source competency models from other sources and then just use them as they are without further modification. In the community college workforce development world, that might include examining existing community college competency studies. One example might be the leadership competency study that was researched by the American Association of Community Colleges (AACC) (American Association of Community Colleges 2013)—or one study that specifically targeted an examination of workforce development competencies for community college educators (Gerity 1998). A second example are the competencies identified by the National Association of Workforce Development Professionals (National Association of Workforce Development Professionals 2018). A third is that community college workforce developers could use competency studies related to the field—such as the talent development capability study conducted by the Association for Talent Development (ATD) (Arneson, Rothwell, & Naughton 2013; Galagan, Hirt, & Vital 2019).

The second way is to source competency models from other sources and then modify them to fit the unique needs of a specific community college workforce development function. As a simple example, one community college could seek copyright permission from AACC or ATD to use their studies but form research teams to customize those competency studies to fit the specific requirements of one community college in one geographic location (Arneson, Rothwell, & Naughton 2013). Another example would be the U.S. DOL Competency Model Peer Learning Group (PLG). PLG is an interactive forum for education and workforce professionals who are using (or looking to use) industry competency models in talent conversations with businesses (https://www.careeronestop.org/CompetencyModel/). The latter process could be done in many ways—such as focus groups, interviews, surveys, and other approaches.

The third way is to follow rigorous approaches to building corporate-culture-specific competency studies (Rothwell, Graber, Dubois, Zabellero, Haynes, Alkhalaf, & Sager 2015; Rothwell & Lindholm 1999). There is more than one correct way to do that (Dubois 1993). A typical approach is to begin with Behavioral Event Interviews (BEI). A BEI is a form of qualitative research in which experienced practitioners are interviewed and are asked such questions as these:

- Tell me a story about the most difficult situation you ever faced in your work in this organization.
- What happened step-by-step?
- What were you thinking, feeling and doing as it occurred?
- When and where did this situation happen?
- Who was involved? Please provide job titles, not names.
- What made the situation so difficult?

The interview results are qualitatively analyzed for common themes, and those themes are competencies. Competencies are typically made measurable by behaviors or work results, and those must sometimes be separately investigated. BEIs, because they focus on workers' past experiences, tend to be past-focused.

Competency models can become the foundation of entire HR systems (Dubois & Rothwell 2004). They can thus be used to recruit, select, onboard, train, develop, appraise, manage, reward, and even promote workers. They can be paired with job descriptions, which describe the work to be performed.

TRENDS SHAPING THE FUTURE

A *trend* is, of course, a prevailing tendency. It can center around, among other things, the work, the workers, the workplace, and the work environment. The *work* is what is done to achieve results; the *workers* are the actors who perform the work and secure results; the *workplace* is the organizational setting or context within which people do their work; and, the *work environment* is the world outside organizations that shape workplaces, workers, and work.

Consider trends in the *work*:

- More people want to work from home rather than in workplaces.
- More work is done online and less work is done manually.
- Full-time jobs are going away in favor of project-based work that is focused on producing specific results or deliverables.
- More work will be performed by artificial intelligence (AI), and many jobs will go away because the work can be more effectively performed by AI.

Consider trends with *workers*:

- The global population is aging.
- Fewer young people are available to recruit for entry-level positions due to a globally aging population.
- People are living longer, and that means more elderly people are in the workforce.
- Employers will be forced to examine traditionally overlooked labor groups such as retirees and the disabled due to labor shortages.
- Immigration is necessary due to declining birth rates in many nations.
- Robots are entering the workforce and will create new issues about worker rights and human-robot interactions.

Consider trends with workplaces:

- More research is available on how to create physical work environments that are conducive to worker performance.
- Employers have much information available about how to set up offices to support productivity.
- Less research is available on creating effective home offices than residential offices.

Each trend above, and many others, will shape the future conditions that affect workforce development in community colleges. Many organizations study trends. One excellent source is the World Futures Society (WFS).

HOW CAN THE FUTURE COMPETENCIES NEEDED BY WORKFORCE DEVELOPMENT PRACTITIONERS BE IDENTIFIED AND USED?

Competency models can be made future-focused if competency identification begins with a study of future trends and then invites experienced workers and decision-makers to reflect on:

- What trends are shaping the future of work, the workforce and the workplace?
- How are those trends defined in your organizational setting?
- How important are those trends?
- What are likely causes of the trends?
- What will be the probable results or consequences of the trends?
- What strategic plans will organizations need to address those unfolding trends?
- What competencies will be needed by managers and by workers to implement the strategic plans?
- How can those competencies be measured or assessed?
- How can those competencies be developed over time?
- How can the competencies be selected for?
- How can demonstration of the competencies be evaluated?

Use the worksheet appearing at the end of the chapter to work through these questions in one community college to align competencies with organizational strategy (see table 14.1).

The results of this kind of competency modeling effort will provide the foundation for a future-oriented competency model. It can be geared to the leadership role of Workforce Development in a Community College. Alternatively, it can be geared to one or more staff roles.

CONCLUSION

Competencies can provide a foundation for planning for the future of secondary workforce development staffing. That can be essential to paint the way forward to execute strategic plans for community colleges.

Table 14.1. A Worksheet to Plan for Future Competencies of Community College Workforce Development Educators

Directions: Use this worksheet to plan for the future competencies of postsecondary community college workforce development educators. For each question appearing above a column below, provide your answers in the space(s) provided. Add space as needed. There are no "right" or "wrong" answers in any absolute sense, but there are some answers that may be more visionary or better than others.

What trends are shaping the future of work, the workforce and the workplace?	How are those trends defined in your organizational setting?	How important are those trends?	What are the likely causes of the trends?	What will be the probable results or consequences of the trends?	What strategic plans will organizations need to address those unfolding trends?	What competencies will be needed by managers and by workers to implement the strategic plans?	How can those competencies be measured or assessed?	How can those competencies be developed over time?	How can the competencies be selected for?	How can demonstration of the competencies be evaluated?
1										
2										
3										
4										
5										
6										
7										
8										
9										
10										

REFERENCES

American Association of Community Colleges. *AACC Competencies for Community College Leaders*. 2nd ed. Washington: American Association of Community Colleges, 2013.

Arneson, Justin, Rothwell, William J., & Naughton, Jennifer. *ASTD Competency Study: The Training and Development Profession Revisited*. Alexandria, VA: ASTD Press, 2013.

Dubois, David. *Competency-Based Performance Improvement*. Amherst, MA: HRD Press, 1993.

Dubois, David, and Rothwell, William J. *Competency-Based Human Resource Management*. Palo Alto, CA: Davies-Black Publishing, 2004.

Galagan, Pat, Hirt, Morgean, and Vital, Courtney. *Capabilities for Talent Development: Shaping the Future of the Profession*. Alexandria, VA: Association for Talent Development, 2019.

Gerity, Patrick. "Competencies for Community College Workforce Training and Development Professionals," *The Catalyst* 28, no. 2 (1998), 5–6 & 11.

National Association of Workforce Development Professionals. *CWDP Competencies*, 2018. https://cdn.ymaws.com/www.nawdp.org/resource/resmgr/Certification/2018_CWDP_Competencies.pdf

Rothwell, William, Graber, James, Dubois, David, Zabellero, Aileen, Haynes, Catherine, Alkhalaf, Ali, & Sager, Sarah. *The Competency Toolkit*. 2nd ed. 2 vols. Amherst, MA: HRD Press, 2015.

Rothwell, W., & Lindholm, J. "Competency Identification, Modeling and Assessment in the USA." *International Journal of Training and Development* 3 no. 2 (1999), 90–105.

Appendix A

Rating Your Competence in Workforce Development

Directions: Use this instrument to rate how important specific workforce development competencies are to you and how much you need professional development. In the first column, review the list of competencies; in the second column, rate how important those competencies are to you in your job at present; in the third column, rate how important professional development is to you; and, finally, in the fourth and final column, multiply the ratings of columns 2 and 3. The product of the multiplied scores will indicate the relative weighting of importance and need for development. Use the highest ratings as the basis to prioritize your professional development needs for the next year.

	Workforce Development Competencies	How Important Are the WD Competencies to Your Job?					What Is Your Personal Need for Professional Development?					Importance X Need for Development (Weighting)
		1	2	3	4	5	1	2	3	4	5	
1	**Training and Organization Development*** Analyzes training needs; designs and develops learning experiences; delivers instruction; evaluates instruction; builds effective corporate culture	1	2	3	4	5	1	2	3	4	5	
2	**Leadership** Influences others; effects change; sustains change	1	2	3	4	5	1	2	3	4	5	
3	**Client Management and Relations** Builds relationships with clients inside the organization; maintains relationships with others	1	2	3	4	5	1	2	3	4	5	
4	**Internal Relations** Builds relationships with clients outside the	1	2	3	4	5	1	2	3	4	5	

Appendix A

organization; maintains relationships with other departments within the institution

5 **Communication Skills**
Writes effectively; speaks effectively; listens effectively

	1	2	3	4	5		1	2	3	4	5

6 **Recruiting, Hiring and Orienting**
Sources talent; selects effective workers; helps orient newcomers, making them productive as quickly as possible

	1	2	3	4	5		1	2	3	4	5

7 **Personal Organization and Office Management**
Uses time management effectively; works with others; manages computer and other equipment

	1	2	3	4	5		1	2	3	4	5

8 **Financial Management/ Budgeting**
Sets up accounts within the organization's guidelines; creates budgets; tracks budgets; maintains paper trail for money spent

	1	2	3	4	5		1	2	3	4	5

9	**Program Planning and Learning Design** Establishes effective courses; follows rules of the institution; creates syllabi and other instructional documents; ensures effective instructional delivery standards are followed	1	2	3	4	5	1	2	3	4	5
10	**Marketing and Promoting Programs** Sources clients; develops and implements effective marketing campaigns through social media and traditional media such as websites, newspapers, bulletin boards	1	2	3	4	5	1	2	3	4	5
11	**Professional Development for Self and Others** Develops self; mentors others; coaches others; develops staff	1	2	3	4	5	1	2	3	4	5
12	**Supervision and Management** Provides effective oversight of staff members reporting to him or her; provides daily	1	2	3	4	5	1	2	3	4	5

Appendix A

guidance and feedback to staff members

13 **External and Community Relations** 1 2 3 4 5
Establishes relationships with individuals and groups outside the institution; participates in community groups; makes active efforts to link the institution/college with community groups

14 **Program Support** 1 2 3 4 5
Ensures staff members have the time, money, supervision, and people necessary to do their jobs; clarifies priorities

Appendix B

Selected Resources for Community College Workforce Development Professionals

This Appendix lists selected resources of use by community college workforce development professionals.

CONTENTS OF THIS APPENDIX

- *Selected Associations and Conferences*
- *Selected Educational Degree Program Providers for Workforce Development*
- *Selected Educational Certificate Program Providers for Workforce Development*
- *Selected Certification Programs*
- *Selected Journals*
- *Selected Websites*
- *Selected Books*
- *Selected Videos*
- *Other Selected Resources*

SELECTED ASSOCIATIONS AND CONFERENCES

AACC Workforce Development Institute. https://www.aacc.nche.edu/programs/workforce-economic-development/wdi2018/
Academy of Human Resource Development. https://www.ahrd.org/
American Association of Community Colleges. https://www.aacc.nche.edu/
Association for Talent Development. https://www.td.org/

International Society for Performance Improvement. www.ispi.org
Organization Development Network. https://www.odnetwork.org/
Society for Human Resource Management. https://www.shrm.org/
The University Council for Workforce and Human Resource Education. http://www.theuniversitycouncil.org/?page_id=17

SELECTED EDUCATIONAL DEGREE PROGRAM PROVIDERS FOR WORKFORCE DEVELOPMENT

Indiana University of Pennsylvania. Career and Technical Education. https://iup.edu/careerteched/
Ohio State University. Workforce Development and Education. https://ehe.osu.edu/educational-studies/wde/
Penn State University. Workforce Education and Development. Offers onsite and online degrees. https://ed.psu.edu/lps/workforce-ed
Southern Illinois University. Workforce Education and Development. https://ehs.siu.edu/wed/
Temple University. Career and Technical Education. https://bulletin.temple.edu/undergraduate/education/career-technical-education/
University of Georgia. Workforce Education. Offers onsite and online degrees. https://coe.uga.edu/academics/degrees/phd-workforce-education

SELECTED EDUCATIONAL CERTIFICATE PROGRAM PROVIDERS FOR WORKFORCE DEVELOPMENT

Louisiana State University. Graduate Certificate in Workforce Development. https://online.lsu.edu/online-degree-programs/graduate-certificate/workforce-development/

SELECTED CERTIFICATION PROGRAMS

Association for Talent Development (ATD). Certified Professional in Learning and Performance (CPLP). https://www.td.org/certification
International Society for Performance Improvement. Certified Performance Technologists (CPT). https://www.ispi.org/certification
National Association of Workforce Development Professionals. Certified Workforce Development Professional (CWDP). https://www.nawdp.org/page/AboutCWDP

SELECTED JOURNALS

HRMagazine. https://www.shrm.org/hr-today/news/hr-magazine/fall2019/Pages/default.aspx
International Journal of Training and Development. https://onlinelibrary.wiley.com/journal/14682419
International Journal of Vocational Education and Training Research. http://www.ijvetr.org/
Journal of Vocational Education and Training. https://tandfonline.com/toc/rjve20/current
Journal for Workforce Education and Development. https://opensiuc.lib.siu.edu/ojwed/
List of selected journals. http://guides.libraries.psu.edu/aed/journals
Performance and Improvement. https://ispi.org//ISPI/Resources/Performance_Improvement_Journal.aspx
Performance Improvement Quarterly. https://onlinelibrary.wiley.com/journal/19378327
TD at work. https://www.td.org/td-at-work
Workforce Education Forum. https://ed.psu.edu/ppdc/workforce-education-forum

Appendix B 169

SELECTED WEBSITES

Career One Stop. https://www.careeronestop.org/
The Competency Clearinghouse. https://www.careeronestop.org/CompetencyModel/
The DACUM Clearinghouse. http://www.dacum.org/
The Dictionary of Occupational Titles. https://occupationalinfo.org/
ERIC Clearinghouse on Adult, Career, and Vocational Education . [Columbus, Ohio: The Clearinghouse, 199-?] Software, E-Resource. https://lccn.loc.gov/2001561959.
ERIC Clearinghouse on Adult, Career, and Vocational Education . [Columbus, Ohio: The Clearinghouse, 199-?] Software, E-Resource. https://www.calpro-online.org/ERIC/Index.asp
ERIC Clearinghouse on Adult, Career, and Vocational Education . [Columbus, Ohio: The Clearinghouse, 199-?] Software, E-Resource. https://eric.ed.gov/
Work Keys Practice Test. https://www.test-guide.com/free-workkeys-practice-tests.html

SELECTED BOOKS

Gray, Kenneth. (Ed.) *Other Ways to Win: Creating Alternatives for High School Graduates* . 3rd ed. Thousand Oaks, CA: Corwin, 2006
Gray, Kenneth & Herr, Edwin. *Workforce Education: The Basics.* London: Pearson, 1997.
Rothwell, William J. and Gerity, Patrick. (Eds.). *Cases in Linking Workforce Development to Economic Development: Community College Partnering for Training, Individual Career Planning, and Community and Economic Development.* Washington: American Association of Community Colleges, 2008.
Rothwell, William J., Gerity, Patrick, & Carraway, Vernon. (Eds.). Community College Leaders on Workforce Development. Lanham, MD: Rowman & Littlefield2, 2017.
Rothwell, William J., Gerity, Patrick, & Gaertner, Elaine. Linking Training to Performance: A Guide for Workforce Development Professionals. Washington: American Association of Community Colleges, 2004. Download at https://files.eric.ed.gov/fulltext/ED485869.pdf
Short, S., & Harris, R. *Workforce Development: Strategies and Practices* . New York: Springer, 2014.

SELECTED VIDEOS

Central Piedmont Community College. Central Piedmont's Strategic Planning Process. https://www.youtube.com/watch?v=33RNHv69Fss
Community Colleges Role in America's Workforce Development. https://www.youtube.com/watch?v=IyyMnVJIGSY
Workforce Development Is Talent Development. https://www.youtube.com/watch?v=m3NyiUGlfsc
Workforce training programs at Thomas Nelson Community College. https://www.youtube.com/watch?v=oBeEnvXWZVA

OTHER SELECTED RESOURCES

Strategic Planning for Workforce Development

Creating a workforce development plan. https://www.esri.com/library/brochures/pdfs/creating-a-workforce-plan.pdf
Diablo Valley College. www.dvc.edu/about/governance/college-plans/pdfs/WEDMasterPlan-2015-2020.pdf

Illinois Community College Board. Workforce education strategic plan. http://www.iccb.org/iccb/wp-content/pdfs/workforce/WESP.pdf
Minnesota. https://www.workforcedevelopmentinc.org/about/strategic-plan/
North Dakota State Government. https://www.workforce.nd.gov/workforce/StrategicPlanforWorkforceDevelopment/

Marketing Community College Workforce Development

The Evolving World of Community Colleges. Market Position. https://evolllution.com/resources/
Manchester Community College. https://www.mccnh.edu/wdc
Northshore Technical Community College. Workforce Development. https://www.northshorecollege.edu/programs/workforce-development/index
Truckee Meadows Community College. Instructor success: Marketing strategies. https://www.tmcc.edu/workforce-development-community-education/teachforus/marketing-strategies

Offering Consulting

The Community College Workforce Alliance (CCWA). John Tyler Community College and Reynolds Community College. https://ccwatraining.org/consulting-services/
Edmonds Community College. www.edcc.edu/workforce

Writing Proposals and Contracts

Agreement for Consulting and Training Services. https://corporate.findlaw.com/contracts/operations/agreement-for-consulting-and-training-services-sagent.html
Consulting Proposal Template. https://www.wikihow.com/Sample/Consulting-Proposal-Template
Free Proposal Templates. http://templatelab.com/consulting-proposal-templates/#Consulting_Proposal_Templates
Santa Fe Community College. Proposal for a New Course to be Taught on Campus. https://www.sfcc.edu/continuing-education-course-proposal-form/
Writing a Successful Proposal. https://www.babson.edu/media/babson/assets/teaching-research/writing-a-successful-proposal.pdf

Working with Clients

Project Planning for Training. Centers for Disease Control. www2a.cdc.gov/cdcup/library/templates/CDC_UP_Training_Plan_Template.doc

Evaluating Training

Creating Custom Course Evaluations. University of Pennsylvania. https://www.ctl.upenn.edu/creating-custom-course-evaluations
Survey Monkey. Sample Training Evaluation Template. https://www.surveymonkey.com/mp/training-course-evaluation-survey-template/

Capturing Testimonials from Delighted Clients

12 Testimonial Page Examples You'll Want to Copy. https://blog.hubspot.com/service/testimonial-page-examples

Index

AACC. *See* American Association of Community Colleges
AATN. *See* Arizona Advanced Technology Network
Adecco, 73
adjunct faculty, 23, 29
Advanced Robotics for Manufacturing (ARM), 66, 69; assistance from, 70
advisory boards, 9, 19, 23, 24, 26
African American/Latino student retention: anti-deficit thinking and, 124; conclusion, 131–139; constructive relationships for, 132; Cultural Climate Survey for, 132–139; deficit thinking and, 124; educational persistence and, 125–127; factors of influence, 124, 125; financial persistence and, 127; grants/loan programs for, 127; growth initiatives for, 130–131; human capital investment in, 127–128; Meyerhoff Scholars Program for, 129–130; non-cognitive development and, 124, 125; overview, 123; program modeling for, 129–130; risks for, 127; SES and, 127; in STEM, 130; success with, 126; workforce landscape and, 128
aging population, 141, 156
AH. *See* allied health programs
AI. *See* artificial intelligence
allied health programs (AH), 89–90
alternate apprenticeship (AltA), 82

Amazon HQ2, 9
Amazon Web Services (AWS), 8
American Association of Community Colleges (AACC), 78, 154–155
American Dream, 73
andragogy, 68
anti-deficit thinking, 124
Aoun, Joseph, 42
Apple, 153
apprenticeships, 86; AltA, 82; benefits of, 91–95; completion of, 94; costs of, 93, 94; drawbacks of, 92; employment and, 91, 94, 107n15; in European guilds, 85; faculty for, 95; flexibility in, 93; master/disciple relationships, 85; matching function in, 102; partnership in, 98–99; RA, 82, 87, 88–89, 91; retention in, 92; turnover in, 93; WBL, 81–82, 83, 86
Arizona Advanced Technology Network (AATN), 43
ARM. *See* Advanced Robotics for Manufacturing
artificial intelligence (AI), 85, 141, 156
ASAHP. *See* Association of Schools of Allied Health Professions
assessment: in community college agility building, 30–31, 37; Ivy Tech Community College plan, 30–31; of organizational circles, 59–60; self-assessment, 60; of WBL, 84; by Work

171

Keys, 147–148, 151
assistantship, 86
Association for Career and Technical Education, 78
Association for Talent Development (ATD), 154–155
Association of Schools of Allied Health Professions (ASAHP), 90
ATD. *See* Association for Talent Development
audits, 116–117
autopsy information, 117
AWS. *See* Amazon Web Services

baby boomers, 141, 143
Balanced Scorecard (Kaplan and Norton), 27
Balance Sheet, 112–113
Beere, Carole A., 25
Behavioral Event Interview (BEI), 155
Bensimon, Estela Mara, 59
big fish mentality, 21–22
birth dearth, 42
Black and Latino Male Empowerment group, 124
Blount, David, 19
boundary spanner, 100–101, 106. *See also* success coach
Brookings Institution, 48
Brown, Katie, 21
budgets. *See* finance and budgeting process

C2ER. *See* Council for Community and Economic Research
career services, 6, 19, 70
Carl D. Perkins Act, 62
Carnevale, Anthony, 42
CETF. *See* Clinical Education Task Force
Chamber of Commerce Foundation, U.S., 73, 74
Clinical Education Task Force (CETF), 90
clinical practice, 86
cloud computing, 41
coaching: success coach, 101; WBL and, 83
collaboration: collaborative learning, 130; with employers, 90; in internships, 87; in mentoring, 101; NC3 model, 77; with stakeholders, 86; technological opportunity and, 45; for workforce development equity, 61–62
communication: in community partnerships, 18, 20, 22; equity and, 60; face-to-face interaction, 105; measurement of, 45; skills, 131; with stakeholders, 60; WBL focus, 96, 99–100, 103, 105
community colleges: credit and noncredit programs, 71; LMI and, 5; skills needed in, 153; talent for, 71; technological change and, 69–70; technological opportunity and, 42; workforce skills in, 17. *See also* community colleges, agility building; Gateway Technical College; Ivy Tech Community College; Northern Virginia Community College; Pima Community College
community colleges, agility building: assessment in, 30–31, 37; conclusion, 37–38; early wins in, 36–37; during first year, 35–36; Ivy Tech Community College case study, 29; mission, values, goals in, 32; overview, 27–28; readiness factors for, 28; strategic plan refresh in, 36
community partnerships: adjunct faculty and, 23; advisory boards for, 24, 26; big fish mentality and, 21–22; communication in, 18, 20, 22; conclusion, 25; mutual interest in, 24, 26; overview, 17–18; parameters for, 23–24; pathway for, 25; rules of engagement for, 18–21, 20; time spent for, 24, 26; toolbox for, 24; types of, 19
competencies: conclusion, 157; definitions for, 154; for finance and budgeting process, 119; identification and use of, 154–155; identification and use of future, 157, 158; overview, 153–154; sources of models, 154–155; for strategic partnerships, 12–14; trends in, 155–156; as worker descriptions, 154
Competitive Forces (Porter), 27
consumption, 4–5
convener, 97–98, 105
cooperative education, 86
costs: of apprenticeships, 93, 94; for WBL, 82

Council for Community and Economic Research (C2ER), 4, 5
counseling centers, 129, 130
"Crafting Strategy" (Mintzberg), 38
credit and noncredit programs, 71
critical observation, 131
CRM. *See* customer relationship management
Cultural Climate Survey, 132–139
cultural interaction, 130
customer relationship management (CRM), 104

data-driven decision-making, 3
Davis, R. B., 139
Deal, Terrence, 46
debt, 7, 84, 85, 114, 115
decision-making, 3, 154, 157
deficit thinking, 124
demand-driven model, 88
Department of Labor, U.S., 78, 89, 128; grants from, 115; survey by, 92, 93
depreciation, 113, 114
disabled, 156
diversity, 57–58
dropouts, 127
Dual Enrollment programming, 20

economic development: Pima Community College and, 43, 44; technological opportunity and, 44
Educate to Innovate campaign, 128
effectuation logic, 13, 16
embedded certifications: conclusion, 77–78; NC3 case study, 74–76; NC3 test results, 76–77; tactical approach to, 73–74
employers: collaboration with, 90; employer-led education, 74; as end customer, 74; engagement of, 18; expectation of, 37; needs of, 6, 7, 8, 14, 45, 53, 131, 144; network partnerships and, 74; partnerships, 74; relationships with, 3, 19; training and, 148; value creation and, 74
employment, 4, 117, 141, 150; apprenticeships and, 91, 94, 107n15; barriers to, 144; FAME model and, 105; opportunities, 6, 77, 145; recidivism, 150; skills for, 148; technological opportunity and, 41; WBL and, 84, 86, 95, 102; WIOA and, 144
empowerment: Black and Latino Male Empowerment group, 124; from technological opportunity, 46–47
entrepreneurs, 86; as pipelines, 22
equity: assessment of organizational circles, 59–60; audits and gaps, 59; college and industry collaboration for, 61–62; communication and, 60; mindedness, 59; stakeholders in, 60–61; tools for understanding, 59–62. *See also* workforce development, equity and
experiential learning, 86; faculty in, 99–100; theory and practice in, 99
externship, 86

face-to-face interaction, 105
faculty: adjunct faculty, 23, 29; for apprenticeships, 95; in experiential learning, 99–100; WBL and, 83
Federation of Advanced Manufacturing Excellence (FAME model), 105
fellowship, 86, 93
field-work, 86
finance and budgeting process: budget documents in, 115–116; competencies for, 119; conclusion, 118–119; improvement mindset for, 117–118; knowledge of financial statements in, 111–115; market understanding for, 109–111, 110; operation monitoring, 116–117; overview, 109
financial persistence, 127
financial statements: Balance Sheet, 112–113; in finance and budgeting process, 111–115; Income Statement, 111–112; Statement of Cash Flows, 113–115
flexibility, 13, 14, 93
Flores, Antonio, 131
Fourth Industrial Revolution, 41
Friedman, Thomas, 27
functional stakeholders, 36
Future Shock (Toffler), 67–68

Gates, Bill, 153

Gateway Technical College, 75, 76; Career Pathway, 77, 78; mission of, 78–79; partnerships, 77
Gelsinger, Pat, 41
global workforce needs, 61
grants/loan programs, 127
Great Recession, 27, 29, 42, 88
Guided Pathways/Meta-Majors model, 62

Harper, S. R., 124
Higher Learning Commission (HLC), 42
Hispanic Association of Colleges and Universities, 131
HLC. *See* Higher Learning Commission
Hrabowski, Freeman, 129
human capital investment, 127–128
human capital pipeline, 44

IBM, 153
immigration, 156
inclusion, 57–58, 131
Income Statement, 111–112
incumbent workers, 71
Indiana Career Council, 29
industry-sector models, 82–83
industry stakeholders, 11
Inside Higher Ed, 75
Internet of Things, 41
internships, 86; collaboration in, 87; paid and non-paid, 89; in WBL, 83, 87, 89
Ivy Tech Community College: agility building case study, 29; assessment plan of, 30–31; Simplex implementation, 30; strategic plan of, 33, 34, 35; wet cement plan of, 32–34

job descriptions, 14, 154, 155
Jobs, Steve, 153
job shadowing, 86
job-skills, 75

Kaplan, Robert, 27
Kauffman Foundation, 22
Keller, Helen, 17
Kennedy, Allan, 46
Kissinger, Henry, 67
knowledge management, 82, 101–102
Knowles, Malcolm, 67, 68

labor market information (LMI): collection, analysis, reporting, consumption of, 4–5; community colleges and, 5; conclusion, 8–9; definition of, 3–4; examples of, 4; NOVA and, 3, 5–9; types of, 4; for WBL, 95–96, 104
labor participation, 110
labor shortages, 156
language skills, 131
Latinos, 151. *See also* African American/Latino student retention
leadership skills, 131
learning: approach in 21st century, 67–69; collaborative, 130; data for, 7–8; PLG, 155; principles of adult, 68; service learning, 86; technological change and, 65–66. *See also* experiential learning; Work-Based Learning; work/learn programs
LMI. *See* labor market information

Manpower Group, 73
Manufacturing Skill Standards Council, 78
market understanding, 109–111, 110
McKernan, John R., Jr., 73
McKinsey and Co., 41, 45–46
Megatrends (Naisbitt), 68
mentoring, 85, 86; collaboration in, 101; partnerships in, 98; WBL and, 82, 83, 101, 106; WISE method for, 132
Meyerhoff, Jane, 129
Meyerhoff, Robert, 129
Meyerhoff Scholars Program, 129–130
Microsoft, 153
Mintzberg, Henry, 38
mutual interest, 24, 26
Myers, Vernā, 58

Naisbitt, John, 67, 68–69
National Association of Workforce Boards, 78
National Association of Workforce Development Professionals, 154
National Career Readiness Certificate (NCRC), 147, 149
National Coalition of Certification Centers (NC3): case study, 74–76; collaboration model, 77; formation of, 75; mission of,

78; test results, 76–77
National Skill Coalition, 21
NC3. *See* National Coalition of Certification Centers
NCRC. *See* National Career Readiness Certificate
needs analysis: global workforce, 61; for WBL, 96, 98, 104
negotiation, 13
non-cognitive development, 124, 125
North Carolina Department of Commerce, 61
Northern Virginia Community College (NOVA): data for good, business, learning, 7–8; LMI and, 3, 5–9
Norton, David, 27
NOVA. *See* Northern Virginia Community College
nursing, 29, 43; work/learn programs in, 86, 89–90

Obama, Barack, 128, 131
OJT. *See* on-the-job training
online work, 156
on-the-job training (OJT), 86, 146
organizational circles: equity assessment of, 59–60; recruitment of supporters in, 60; self-assessment in, 60; synergy in, 60
organizational placement, 15–16
organizational strategy, 153
organizational structure, 153
Out of School Youth program, 144

P3s. *See* public/private partnerships
partnerships: in apprenticeships, 98–99; in changing face of workforce development, 143–147; of employers, 74; Gateway Technical College, 77; in mentoring, 98; network, 74; P3s, 15; at Pima Community College, 43, 44, 45; supply chain, 74; in WBL, 98–99, 105; win-win, 145–146, 151; for workforce challenges, 144; work/learn programs, 101. *See also* community partnerships; strategic partnerships
Peace Corps, 67
Peer Learning Group (PLG), 155
Pell Grants, 127, 143

Pennsylvania State University, 129
Pima Community College, 47, 48; economic development and, 43, 44; foundational changes in, 42; HLC evaluation visit, 42; human capital pipeline and, 44; partnerships, 43, 44, 45; research in, 43; student services, 43; workforce development plan, 46
Pinchuck, Nick, 74
pipelines: development of, 20; entrepreneurs as, 22; human capital, 44; talent pipeline, 6, 7, 74, 90, 102; training, 54; workforce pipeline, 87, 89, 94, 95
Pittinsky, Matthew, 75
PLG. *See* Peer Learning Group
Porter, Michael, 27
poverty, 142
practicum, 86
problem-solving, 131
productivity, 156
professional relationships, 44–45
project-based work, 156
public/private partnerships (P3s), 15

RA. *See* Registered Apprenticeship
rear-view mirror reports, 96
reentrants, 142, 150–151
Registered Apprenticeship (RA), 82, 87, 88–89, 91
related technical instruction (RTI), 87
relationship development, 130
reporting: of LMI, 4–5; rear-view mirror reports, 96
residency, 86
retirees, 156
return on investment (ROI), 12, 70, 82, 89, 91, 96
Robot-Proof (Aoun), 42
robots, 66, 156. *See also* Advanced Robotics for Manufacturing
ROI. *See* return on investment
ROTC, 130
RTI. *See* related technical instruction
rules of engagement, 18–21

sales skills, 13
SBDC. *See* Small Business Development Center

school-based enterprise, 86
science, technology, engineering, and mathematics (STEM), 128; African American/Latino student retention in, 130; educational curricula, 131; Meyerhoff Scholars Program for, 129
self-appraisal, 131
service learning, 86
SES. *See* socioeconomic status
Silver Tsunami, 141
Simplex, 30
skills gap, 148, 149
Small and Medium sized Manufacturers (SMMs), 65–66; resources for training, 69–70
Small Business Administration, U.S., 22
Small Business Development Center (SBDC), 22
SMMs. *See* Small and Medium sized Manufacturers
Snap on Incorporated, 74–75, 76, 77
Society of Manufacturing Engineers, 78
socioeconomic status (SES), 127
soft skill development, 130
Spaulding, Shayne, 19
special education programs, 127
stakeholders: collaboration with, 86; communication with, 60; community, 16; external, 28, 31, 36, 38; functional, 36; industry, 11; needs of, 12, 13; in workforce development equity, 60–61
Stand up, Take action, Expect results, Put in work (STEP Academy): birth of, 149; for changing face of workforce development, 149–151; for Latino communities, 151; purpose for reentrants, 150; success of, 151; for win-win partnerships, 145
state aid, 115
Statement of Cash Flows, 113–115
Statement of Net Position, 112
STEM. *See* science, technology, engineering, and mathematics
STEP Academy. *See* Stand up, Take action, Expect results, Put in work
storytelling, 96
strategic partnerships: competencies for, 12–14; conclusion, 16; data for, 14–15; organizational placement and, 15–16;

overview, 11
strategic planning, 27–28, 157; in community college agility building, 36; environmental scan for, 30; at Ivy Tech Community College, 33, 34, 35
strategic thinking: for innovative culture, 29; for WBL, 103
student services, 43, 83, 100
student success, in WBL, 83, 84
student support groups, 130
success coach, 101
supply chain partnerships, 74
supply-demand data, 96
supply-side paradigm, 88
Sutphen, Mona, 24

talent pipeline, 6, 7, 74, 102, 104
Talent Pipeline Academy, 104
teamwork, 131
technological change: challenges for community colleges, 69–70; challenges from advanced manufacturing, 66–67; conclusion, 71–72; future prediction for, 67–69; learning and, 65–66
technological opportunity: checklist for, 43–45; collaboration and, 45; community colleges and, 42; conclusion, 47–48; economic development and, 44; employment and, 41; empowerment from, 46–47; internal silos and, 44; interplay between old and new, 45; overview, 41–42; plan for future, 45–46; professional relationships and, 44–45; short and long term, 44; WBL and, 85
time management, 131
Toffler, Alvin, 67–68
Toyota Motor Manufacturing, 105
traineeship, 86
training programs, 69; employers and, 148; failure of, 70; for incumbent workers, 71; maintenance of relevant, 71–72; need for, 131; for new workers, 71; pipeline, 54; resources of SMMs, 69–70; for tech and manufacturing, 71
trends, 68; in competencies, 155–156; as prevailing tendency, 155; study of future, 157; in work, 156; in workers, 156; in workplaces, 156

Index

trust building, 53
TuSimple, 44
tutoring, 85; WBL and, 83

UMBC. *See* University of Maryland, Baltimore County
UNC. *See* University of North Carolina
unemployment, 4, 27, 88, 110, 128
University of Maryland, Baltimore County (UMBC), 129
University of North Carolina (UNC), 129
Urban Institute, 19

Valencia, R. R., 124
value creation, 74
value statement, 96–97, 104
virtual reality (VR), 85
Votruba, James C., 25
VR. *See* virtual reality

Walmart, 153
Walton, Sam, 153
Watson, Tom, 153
WBL. *See* Work-Based Learning
WDBs. *See* workforce development boards
Wells, Gail W., 25
wet cement plan, 32–34
WFS. *See* World Futures Society
wholesale thinking, 97, 105
Williamson, Jimmie, 75
win-win partnerships, 145–146, 151
WIOA. *See* Workforce Innovation and Opportunity Act
WISE method for mentoring, 132
Work-Based Learning (WBL): apprenticeship programs, 81–82, 83, 86; assessment of, 84; best practices, 103, 104–106; boundary spanner in, 100–101, 106; coaching and, 83; common platform in, 103; communication focus in, 96, 99–100, 103, 105; conclusion, 101–103; convener for, 97–98, 105; costs for, 82; defined, 86–88, 103; employment and, 84, 86, 95, 102; faculty and, 83; forms of, 81; implementation of, 95–101; industry-sector models for, 82–83; internships in, 83, 87, 89; labor market data for, 95–96, 104; mentoring and, 82, 83, 101, 106; needs analysis for, 96, 98, 104; overview, 85–86; partnership in, 98–99, 105; relationship building for, 95; scheduling of, 83–84; strategic thinking for, 103; strategies in, 88–95, 103; student services and, 83; student success in, 83, 84; success coach for, 101; technological opportunity and, 85; tips for building, 81–85; track record in, 84; tutoring and, 83; value statement for, 96–97, 104; wholesale thinking for, 97, 105; written agreements and, 84. *See also* work/learn programs
work environment, 156
workers: incumbent, 71; new workers, 71; performance, 156; rights of, 156; trends in, 156; worker descriptions, 154
workforce challenges: advanced manufacturing and, 66, 67; discussions for, 143; partnerships for, 144; solutions for, 145, 151
workforce communities, 142
workforce development, case for: buy-in and, 54; conclusion, 54; data and, 53; documentation of process, 52–53; environment and, 51–52
workforce development, changing face of: conclusion, 151–152; overview, 141–143; partnerships in, 143–147; STEP Academy for, 149–151; Work Keys in, 147–149
workforce development, equity and: conclusion, 62; diversity and inclusion in, 57–58; overview, 57; tools for understanding equity, 59–62
workforce development boards (WDBs), 112, 114, 116, 146
Workforce Innovation and Opportunity Act (WIOA), 61, 62, 144, 146–147
Workforce Investment Act, 61
workforce pipeline, 87, 89, 94, 95
Work Keys: assessment by, 147–148, 151; for businesses, 148; in changing face of workforce development, 147–149; creation of, 147; sill sets matched with, 148–149
work/learn programs, 84, 86, 105; development of, 98; funding for, 94; in nursing, 86, 89–90; partnerships, 101;

stakeholders, 97; workplace liaison in, 100
work readiness classes, 150
World Economic Forum, 41
World Futures Society (WFS), 156
The World is Flat (Friedman), 27

YouTube, 69

About the Editors and Contributors

William J. Rothwell, PhD, SPHR, SHRM-SCP, CPLP Fellow, RODC, FLMI, professor, Workforce Education and Development, The Pennsylvania State University; president, Rothwell & Associates, Inc., State College, PA

Patrick E. Gerity, PhD, chief executive officer, Workforce Resource Network, Bethel Park, PA

Vernon L. Carraway, PhD, chief executive officer, Langston Du Bois Institute, State College, PA

* * *

Bryan Albrecht, EdD, president, Gateway Technical College

Stephen R. Catt, EdD, Deputy Director of Education and Workforce Development, Advanced Robotics for Manufacturing (ARM)

Robin Cole Jr., DSc, dean, Business and Technologies, Southwest Tennessee Community College, Memphis, TN

Alex Cooley, MPA, manager, Labor Market Information Services, Northern Virginia Community College

Angela Davis, MBA, special assistant for Equity & Inclusion, Office of the President, Durham Technical Community College

Sue Ellspermann, PhD, president, Ivy Tech Community College

Alicia R. Hooks, PhD, executive director, Dr. Thomas R. Burke Educational Center, Entrepreneurship & Workforce Center, Kansas City Kansas Community College

Matt Janisin, EdD, vice president, Business and Workforce Solutions, Gateway Technical College

Lee D. Lambert, PhD, JD, chancellor, Pima Community College

Jairo McMican, MS, dean of Student Learning, Central Carolina Community College

Susan Paris, MEd, chief academic officer/vice president of Academics and Guided Career Pathways, Durham Technical Community College

Victor Rodgers, MBA, associate provost, Harrisburg Area Community College

Paul Schreffler, D.M., vice chancellor, Economic and Workforce Solutions (retired), Kentucky Community College and Technical College System

Ty A. Stone, PhD, president, Jefferson Community College

John Will, EdD, president, Wisconsin Indianhead Technical College

Michael C. Wood, PhD, internship coordinator, Marymount University

Made in the USA
Coppell, TX
14 January 2024